IMAGES
of America

BOONE

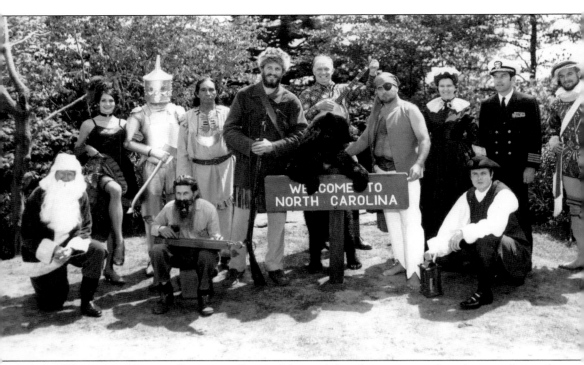

WELCOME, NORTH CAROLINA STYLE. Many of the characters in this photograph are from High Country attractions. Performers from the Wizard of Oz, Horn in the West, and Tweetsie Railroad join pirates, musicians, colonists, Santa, and pioneers. (Courtesy Jerry Burns with *The Blowing Rocket*.)

(*On the Cover*) This photograph shows a bustling downtown Boone in 1947. The movie, *West of Sonora*, is playing at the Appalachian Theatre, a historic theatre and mainstay of downtown. (Courtesy University Archives and Records, Appalachian State University.)

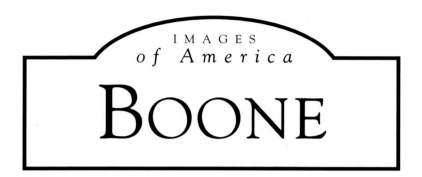

IMAGES
of America

BOONE

Donna Akers Warmuth

ARCADIA
PUBLISHING

Published by Arcadia Publishing
Charleston, South Carolina

Printed in the United States of America

Library of Congress Catalog Card Number: 2003106340

For all general information contact Arcadia Publishing at:
Telephone 843-853-2070
Fax 843-853-0044
E-mail sales@arcadiapublishing.com
For customer service and orders:
Toll-Free 1-888-313-2665

Visit us on the Internet at www.arcadiapublishing.com

CONTENTS

ACKNOWLEDGMENTS

This collection of photographs and postcards of Boone, North Carolina, tells the story of its development from a "lost province" to the thriving retail and arts center it is today. The volume is not intended to be a formal, thorough history of the town, but it is a documentation using images of the past that depict many changes in Boone's development.

This book would not have been possible without the generosity of many community people. The Historic Boone group, active until a few years ago, allowed the author to use many images from their collection. Dr. Gene Reece, who passed away recently, and Kaye Edmisten, former director of Downtown Boone Development Association, put many hours into researching and developing a collection of Boone history memorabilia. Palmer Blair, who had a photo shop for many years in downtown, likely took many of the photographs used in the book. George Flowers and Paul Weston, other Boone photographers, also probably captured many of these images. Many individuals and organizations answered the requests to share photographs of and information about Boone. Many thanks to the following individuals and groups: Appalachian Cultural Museum, Appalachian State University, *The Blowing Rocket*, Claude Bodenhamer, Boone Chamber of Commerce, Boone Drug, Boone Fire Department, Boone Police Department, Wade E. Brown, Jerry Burns, Armfield Coffey, Daniel Boone Inn, Ronald Elrod, Randy Feimster, George Flowers, Folklore Productions, Sanna Gafney, Brenda Jones Gragg, Virgil and Jennifer Greer, Tim Hagaman, C.J. and Pauline Hayes, Howell Hayes, Evelyn Johnson, Junaluska Heritage Foundation, Brian Lambeth, Red Lyons, Peggy Honeycutt Mains, Louvenia Martin, Pam Mitchem, Rosalee Clawson Norris, Patt Paal, Anna Boyce Phillips, Public Affairs at Appalachian State University, Sarah Blair Spencer, St. Elizabeth Catholic Church , Richard Trexler, University Archives and Records at Appalachian State University, Watauga County Public Library, Watauga County Sheriffs Office, Chris Wilcox, and Iva Dean Winkler. The assistance and advice of Laura New and Kelle Broome of Arcadia Publishing has been essential to the successful completion of this project.

INTRODUCTION

The first inhabitants of the area around Boone were the Cherokee Indians who hunted in these hills. Only archeological sites, with points, pottery, and a few bones, remain from their activity. The buffalo trail, left from migrating herds crossing through Watauga County, Tennessee and Wilkesboro, was used by Native Americans and later by long hunters. This trail provided a way into these high mountains. In 1752, Bishop August Gottlich Spangenberg scouted through the area looking for a site for a Moravian settlement. Due to the harsh weather and steep terrain, Bishop Spangenberg established the settlement in Wilkes County instead. Howard's Knob, a prominent peak above Boone, was named for Ben Howard, a frequent visitor to the area from 1739 to 1769, who brought his cattle up from Yancey County to graze. Daniel Boone, for whom the town was named, passed through the area in 1760 on a hunting expedition. Daniel Boone and his hunting companions used Ben Howard's cabin as a base for their long hunts. The location of the Howard cabin was along present-day Rivers Street. Today, a statue of Daniel Boone and a plaque are all that remain, on Rivers Street near Bodenhamer Drive.

Most of the settlers here were English, Scotch-Irish, and German in ancestry and came to the mountains from the lowlands and the foothills after the Revolutionary War. They crossed by the buffalo trail through gaps, ridges and valleys to search for land, a new way of life, and freedom. Watauga County was established by the North Carolina General Assembly in 1849, from parts of Ashe, Wilkes, Caldwell, and Yancey Counties.

The community that became Boone in 1850 started out as a single row of houses on a street below Howard's Knob and was called Councill's Store. Jordan Councill Jr.'s store, established in 1800 near the corner of King and Depot Streets, was the focus for trade and communication for much of the area. Councill moved goods such as dried fruit, meat, hides, butter, beeswax, and tallow by wagon as far away as Charleston, South Carolina.

In 1850, Council Store had become the Boone Post Office. Although Boone became the county seat, the communities of Valle Crucis, Shulls Mills, and Beaver Dam were also rivals for county seat. The town was chartered in 1872 with a population of about 850 persons. Sawmills were built near the New River to produce lumber to construct buildings in the town.

The first buildings in Boone included the B.J. Crawley store and residence (early 1850s), the Dr. J.G. Rivers house, the James Tatum storehouse, the Blair Hotel (1870), the James W. Councill house, a saloon and blacksmith shop, and the Joseph Councill brick house. W.L. Bryan was named the first mayor of the town. J.W. Councill, Dr. J.G. Rivers, T.J. Hall, and J.B. Todd were appointed to be the first town commissioners. Water Street (originally the Burnsville Highway), Queen Street, and King Street were the original streets.

Boone came through the Civil War with some damage, although not as serious as many Southern towns suffered. Watauga County supplied more than 800 men to the Confederacy.

Although most people sided with the South, some inhabitants did join the Union Army. Gen. George Stoneman engaged with the Home Guard in Boone in 1865, killing several townspeople. After the war and reconstruction, better roads were built and markets for goods expanded. With the construction of the Eastern Tennessee and Western North Carolina Railroad in 1917, one daily train ran from Johnson City and one from Boone, a four-hour trip one way. The train stopped in Sycamore Shoals, Roan Mountain, Cranberry, Montezuma, Linville, and Boone. After this, the import and export markets for Boone were greatly expanded.

In 1899, Watauga Academy was opened by B.B. and D.D. Dougherty, providing education for area youth. The school grew, becoming a training school, a teacher's college, and finally Appalachian State University, adding jobs and money to the town's economy. The telephone system was begun in the county in 1907 as the Watauga Telephone Company.

In 1915, the town had a public library, three churches, one bank, a Masonic Hall and three hotels, electric lights, garages and livery stables, and a population of about 700 people. John Preston Arthur in his *A History of Watauga County* stated, "there is no reason why Boone should not become the best and largest summer resort in the state."

Until the 1920s, Watauga County was a part of an area called the Lost Provinces, which also included Ashe and Allegheny counties. The Lost Provinces were more economically tied to Tennessee, until transportation routes, first the train and then highways, connected it the Piedmont towns.

The 1940s flood was a major disaster in the area, killing several people and destroying crops, roads, and buildings. The lines of the railroad were also washed out and it was not rebuilt. During the 1940s, tourists began to discover Boone and with the opening of Tweetsie Railroad theme park in 1956, the town became a travel destination. The introduction of skiing in the 1960s enabled the town to become a winter tourist destination. As a major tourist destination, Boone struggles with how to accommodate and develop within a geographically limited small valley. Development regulations have been passed to ensure that the community retains its aesthetically pleasing appearance.

REFERENCES

Arthur, John Preston. *A History of Watauga County North Carolina*. 1915, Reprint 1992. Johnson City, TN: The Overmountain Press, 1992.

Blowing Rock Historical Society. *Postcards of Historic Blowing Rock*. Boone, North Carolina: Parkway Publishers, 2002.

Brown, Wade E. *Wade E. Brown: Recollections and Reflections*. Boone, North Carolina: Parkway Publishers, 1997.

Corbitt, Tom, ed. *History of Development of Public Education in Watauga County, North Carolina*, compiled by a Bicentennial Committee.

Currie, Ruth Douglas. *Appalachian State University The First Hundred Years*. Prospect, KY: Harmony House Publishers, 1998.

Dunlap, Bill and Tom Corbitt. *Remembrances. 1974.*

Eggers, Herman. *The Town of Boone, North Carolina: Sketch of the First Hundred Years.*

Horton, Ben. *Glimpses of Yesteryear:Watauga County,1975.*

McFarland, Betty. *Sketches of Early Watauga*. Boone Branch, American Association of University Women, 1973.

Nelson, Lynn. "Daniel Boone-The Town's Namesake," *Watauga Democrat*, March 12, 1999.

Selders, A., editor. *Directory of Boone, North Carolina July, 1925.* reprinted by Historic Boone.

Whitener, Daniel J. *History of Watauga County A Souvenir of Watauga Centennial Boone, North Carolina.* 1949.

One

DOWNTOWN'S CHANGING SCENES

Boone is located in a scenic valley at the base of Howard Knob and Rich Mountain to the north. The elevation is 3,333 feet above sea level, with the mountain peaks reaching another 1,000 to 1,400 feet.

Judge Dudley Farthing of the Watauga County court laid off streets and lots. According to John Preston Arthur in A History of Watauga County, North Carolina, *the main street running east and west was called King Street, and the first street north and parallel to it was named Queen Street. Water Street was designated the street running between the Watauga County Bank Building and the law office of E.S. Coffey. Burnsville Street was the first name for the southern part of Water's Street, as it led south from King Street and between the house of R.C. Rivers and Fletcher and Lovill's law offices in front of the jail.*

The first buildings in Boone included the B.J. Crawley store and residence (early 1850s), the Dr. J.G. Rivers house, the James Tatum storehouse, the Blair Hotel (1870) the James W. Councill house, a saloon and blacksmith shop, and a brick house built by Joseph Councill, which was used as the offices for the Watauga Democrat.

Very few of Boone's earliest buildings remain. Many of them were constructed of logs, and later frame buildings, which were not built to last long. Several fires occurred downtown also, destroying older buildings. Commercial development at several points in history had a "new is better" attitude which resulted in demolition of many older buildings as well. The downtown has no buildings dating before the Civil War. The oldest buildings are the Lovill House (1875), the Jail (1889), and the Council House (1878).

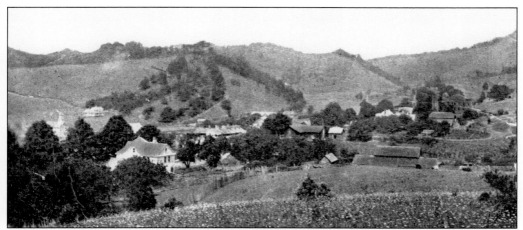

BOONE, NORTH CAROLINA, LOOKING WEST, RICH MOUNTAIN IN BACKGROUND. Postmarked 1911, this postcard shows the cleared and logged ridges even as early as 1911. The brick courthouse, built in 1904, is the large building on the right of the photograph along King Street. The barns and fields bear testimony to the importance of agriculture in Boone's history. (Courtesy Anna Boyce Phillips.)

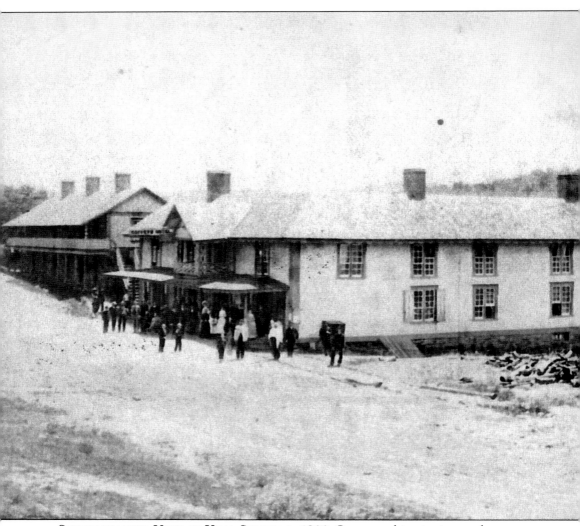

STEREOGRAPHIC VIEW OF KING STREET C. 1900. Stereographic viewing cards were common before the advent of cameras and with the viewer, they almost created a 3-D image. This scene along King Street shows the Bryan home in the background and the Coffey (later the Blair) Hotel in the foreground. Coffey's Hotel was owned by W.C. and T.J. Coffey. Col. William L. Bryan was Boone's first mayor in 1872 and was instrumental in the founding of what has become Appalachian State University. These buildings were located on the corner of King and Depot Streets. This set of cards was photographed by L.A. Ramsour of Morganton, North Carolina and produced by R.E. Lofinck, of Manhattan, Kansas. (Courtesy Historic Boone.)

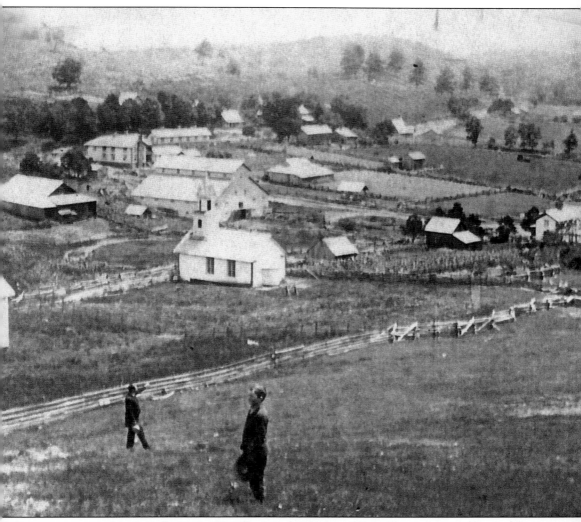

STEREOGRAPHIC VIEW OF PRESENT-DAY RIVERS STREET C. 1900. This stereographic card is an early view of the Boone Baptist Church (white building in the foreground with steeple) and the W.C. Coffey home (the Coffey Hotel) is shown on the left between the two barns. The large white barn with loft was likely the livery stable for the Coffey Hotel. Note the split rail fence in the foreground. The farmhouses and outbuildings show the agricultural base of the early town. (Courtesy Historic Boone.)

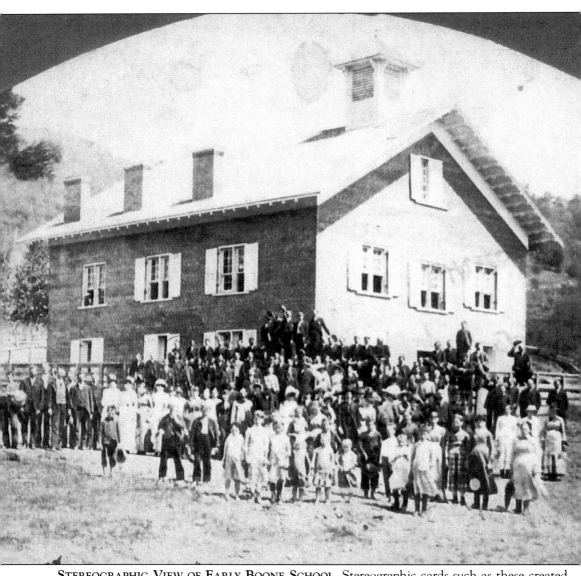

STEREOGRAPHIC VIEW OF EARLY BOONE SCHOOL. Stereographic cards such as these created a 3-D image by using a viewer to see both photographs. This building appears to be an early school or academy in Boone, although nobody can remember its exact location. This may be the Boone Academy, which was established in 1868 near the later Appalachian State University. Since two-story churches were uncommon, local sources believe it to be a school or academy. It is shown on King Street in the background of the photograph on page 13. Schools were important in the area from an early time. In 1899, schools and academies in Watauga County included New River Academy, Cove Creek Academy, Skyland Institute in Blowing Rock, and Watauga Academy. (Courtesy Historic Boone.)

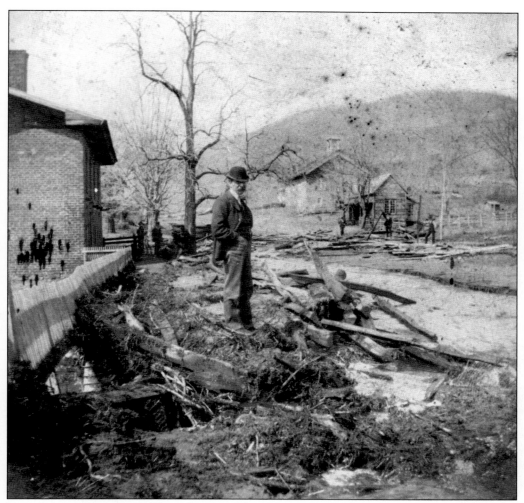

FLOOD OF 1880S ALONG KING STREET. This western view of the south side of King Street shows the devastation of early floods. The building on the left was formerly occupied by the *Watauga Democrat*. The building in the background with the cupola appears to be the first Boone Methodist Church, also shown on page 12. A log cabin and split rail fence are located in front of this building. When the main roads were dirt, heavy rains could make them impassable for days. Also, Boone's location between the mountains and along a stream has created the potential for flooding. (Courtesy Historic Boone.)

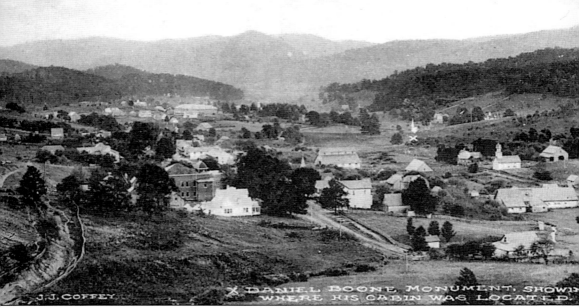

Boone, N. C.   Altitude 3,332 ft.   Highest County Site East of the Rockies.

J. J. COFFEY   X DANIEL BOONE MONUMENT. SHOWN
                                WHERE HIS CABIN WAS LOCATED.

BOONE, NORTH CAROLINA, HIGHEST COUNTY SITE EAST OF THE ROCKIES C. 1915. This early 20th-century eastern view of downtown Boone shows the urbanization that has occurred. It's interesting to note the many different barns in the town. On the left side of the photograph, the white building beside the courthouse is Dr. Little's house. The 1904 brick courthouse can be seen next. The large building in the background in the middle of the postcard appears to be the first Administration building, part of the Appalachian Training School. Note the "x" marking the spot of the Daniel Boone Monument, showing where the Howard cabin was thought to be located. The long white barn on the right was the Coffey Barn. The church with steeple on the right of the image was the first Boone Baptist Church. The commercial development of the town doesn't continue east along King Street past the courthouse, but is primarily houses and farms. Electric lines have been run through town, as evidenced by the utility poles in the foreground. (Courtesy Historic Boone.)

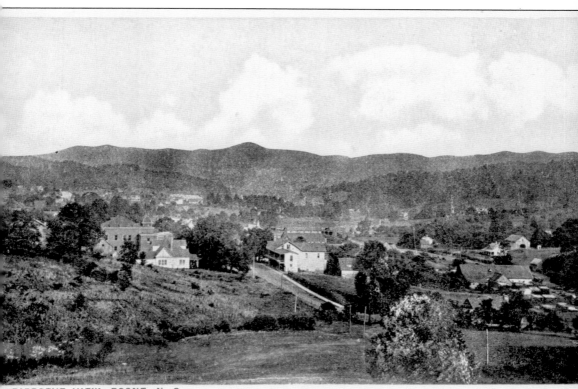

BIRDSEYE VIEW, BOONE, N. C.

BIRD'S EYE VIEW OF BOONE C. 1924. This postcard is the same view as the previous postcard. The Watauga County Courthouse is the large brick building on the left. One of the few differences in the cards is that King Street veers around a mature tree in the above card, and the Boone Baptist Church is no longer on Rivers Street. Dated July 29 1924, the card is addressed to Miss Bug Banner in Butler, Tennessee, and reads, "Lo Bug' This is the good place to have the grand time. Been seeing loads of cute folks. Done got my cap set for an old boy here don't know if I'll get nothing. Love, [illegible name]." Many tourists will agree that Boone and the High Country are places to have a grand time. (Courtesy Brian Lambeth.)

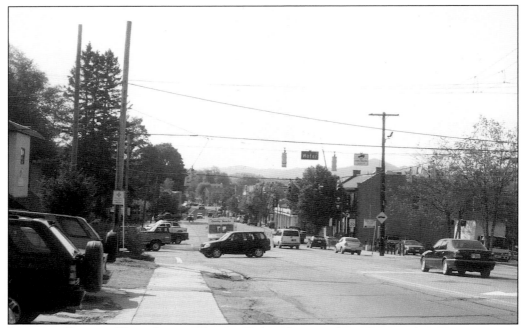

EASTERN VIEW OF KING STREET TODAY. Today, the view from the courthouse appears very changed. This area has become an extension of downtown and contains many offices and commercial uses. No agricultural land or barns remain in downtown. The courthouse was replaced with a modern building. (Courtesy Donna Warmuth.)

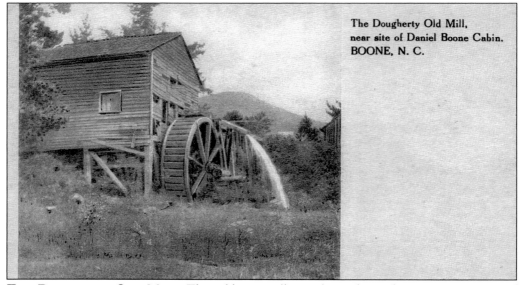

The Dougherty Old Mill, near site of Daniel Boone Cabin. BOONE, N. C.

THE DOUGHERTY OLD MILL. This old gristmill was located on the current campus of Appalachian State University near the Boone cabin site. The mill seems to have the overshot type of water wheel. Early mills were once a popular meeting place, next to courthouses, taverns, and churches. Residents would gather and talk while their corn was ground. This mill was owned by the Dougherty family, founders of Watauga Academy, which would eventually grow into Appalachian State University. (Courtesy Richard Trexler.)

MONUMENT TO DANIEL BOONE, MARKING WHERE HE ONCE LIVED. This postcard shows the monument to Daniel Boone, which was once located near the Faculty Street extension and Duncan Hall on the ASU campus. The monument was constructed in 1912 by Col. William Lewis Bryan at a cost of $203.37. Col. Bryan was a direct descendant of a brother of Boone's wife, Rebecca Bryan. Tradition holds that it was built on the exact site of a log cabin that Daniel Boone used (built by Benjamin Howard) during his hunting trips here. It was inscribed with, "Daniel Boone, Pioneer and Hunter; Born Feb. 11, 1735; Died Sept. 26, 1820." Although arguments were made to preserve it, this marker was replaced with a similar stone marker in 1969 when Faculty Street extension was widened over the site. Original stones from this monument were reportedly saved to construct another monument in the future. The only marker now is a statue of Daniel Boone and a dog near the intersection of Rivers Street and Stadium Drive. (Courtesy Richard Trexler.)

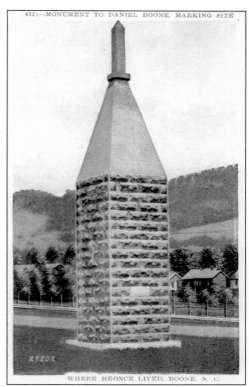

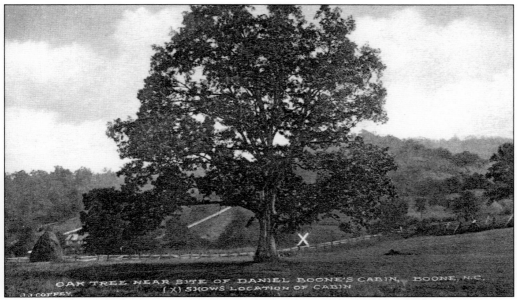

OAK TREE NEAR SITE OF DANIEL BOONE'S CABIN. This photograph was taken prior to the construction of the obelisk monument in 1912. The site of Daniel Boone's cabin was near Duncan Hall and was paved under when Faculty Street Extension was widened in 1969. Note the split-rail fence and haystack in the background. The large tree is no longer at the site. (Courtesy Richard Trexler.)

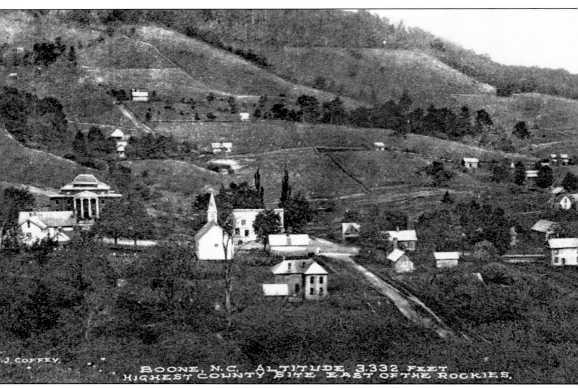

BOONE, N.C. ALTITUDE 3.332 FEET
HIGHEST COUNTY SITE EAST OF THE ROCKIES.

VIEW OF DOWNTOWN BOONE "HIGHEST COUNTY SEAT EAST OF THE ROCKIES." This northern view of downtown Boone, taken after 1904 (due to the presence of the courthouse), shows the older courthouse with a domed roof on the upper side of King Street. On the southern side of King Street, from left to right, are the Blackburn Hotel, the Boone United Methodist Church, and possibly the Lovill law office. Along Depot Street (then Burnesville Road) is the brick jailhouse on the left. The hills surrounding Boone have been logged by this time, leaving a strip of trees along the ridge line. Notice the small houses and outbuildings dotted along the steep slopes. These early settlers were hardy to create a life in such harsh environmental conditions. (Courtesy Richard Trexler.)

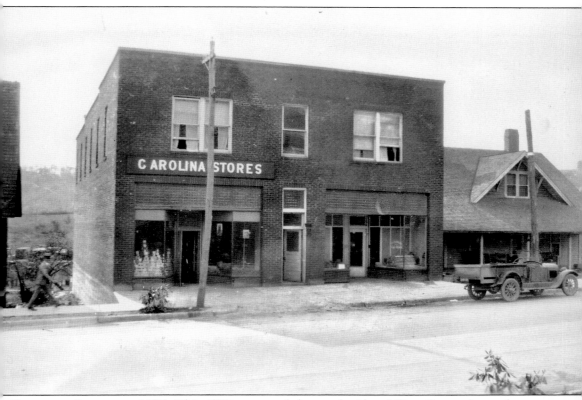

CAROLINA STORES C. 1925. This 1920s scene of the south side of King Street shows the Carolina Stores in the Hahn Building and, next to it, an unknown house, which is no longer there. The Hahn building is now home to Macado's restaurant at 539 W. King Street. Carolina Stores later became a grocery store and then the Winn-Dixie grocery store. (Courtesy Anna Boyce Phillips.)

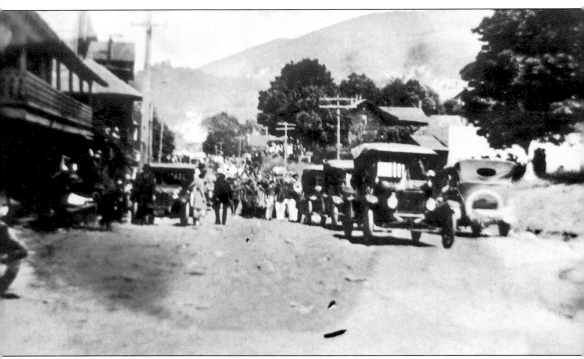

PARADE ON KING STREET C. 1920S. A parade is captured on King Street, looking towards the west. Note the utility lines running along the road. The buildings on the left of the photograph are likely the Blair Hotel and another hotel in the area. On the north side of King Street, the block one contained the Dr. J.W. Jones home and a one-room school. The Model Ts in the parade help date the photograph. Some things never change—this congested scene still occurs in downtown Boone today. (Courtesy Watauga County Public Library.)

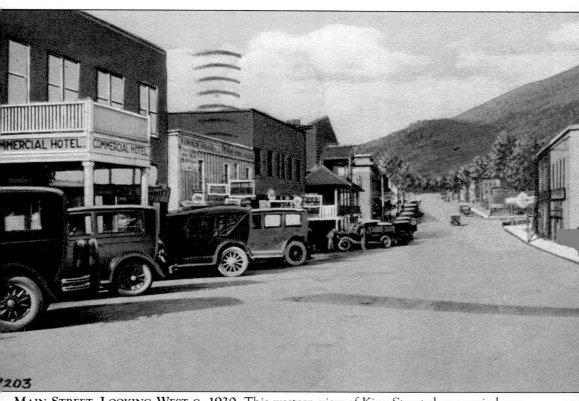

MAIN STREET, LOOKING WEST C. 1930. This western view of King Street shows period cars parked diagonally in front of the Commercial Hotel, which was run by Mr. Falls. This hotel was originally the Blair Hotel. A café market is on the bottom floor. The white frame building next to the hotel is a garage and part of the sign for Boone Drugs can be seen. The building with the veranda was originally the Blair Hotel and later became the Critcher Hotel. The white building in the background on the corner of Depot Street is the Watauga County Bank. On the north side of King Street was a 5&10 store on the corner, as well as Hunt's Department Store, and then the Ed Hodges gas station. (Courtesy Richard Trexler.)

21

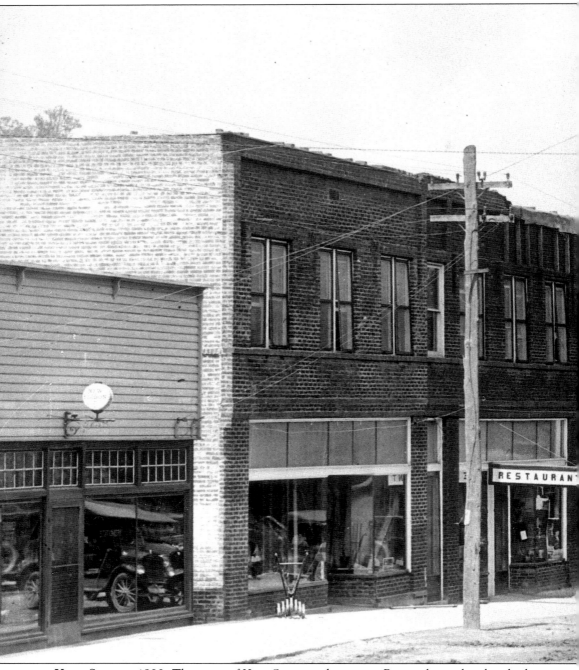

KING STREET, 1923. This view of King Street in downtown Boone shows the already thriving commercial district. King Street doesn't appear to be paved, but is only a dirt road. Businesses pictured, from left to right, are a New Edison car dealership, Qualls Hardware, Carolina Hotel and Restaurant, Ralph Winkler Studebaker, Boone Drug, and the Critcher Hotel. From the corner of Depot Street, one can see the Watauga County Bank (later Northwestern Bank), Farmers Hardware, and the Bryan House. At the time, this was the extent of the business area

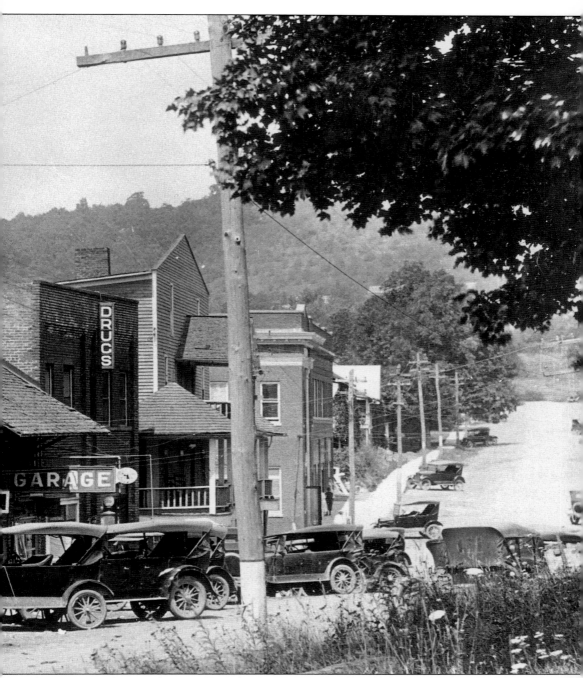

of downtown, with more houses along the western section. The only two businesses in this photograph that are still located downtown are Boone Drug and Farmer's Hardware, which speaks for the importance of medicine and tools. Wade Brown, longtime Boone resident, remembers that the Ralph Winkler Studebaker shop had a drive-in garage in the basement. (Courtesy Historic Boone.)

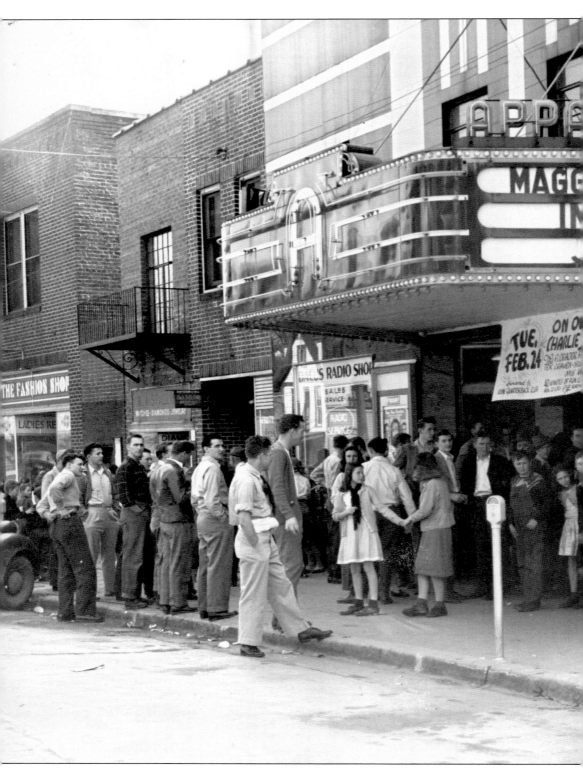

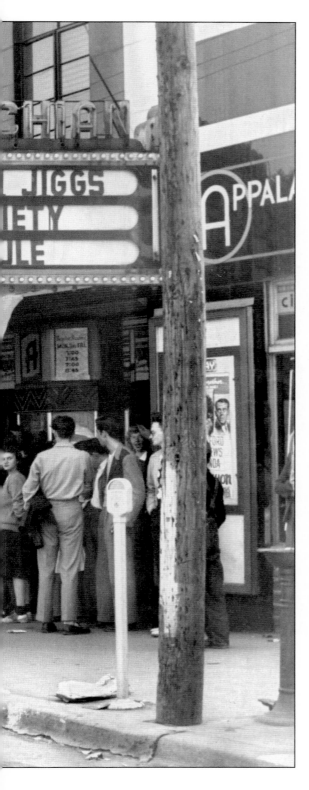

APPALACHIAN THEATRE, EARLY 1950s. The Appalachian Theatre has long been a familiar face in downtown Boone on the block to the east of the intersection of Depot and King Streets. Businesses located to the left of the theatre include Dacus Radio Shop, Stallings Jewelry Store, Dr. E.T. Glenn, Dentist (2nd floor), and the Fashion Shop. The Appalachian Soda Shop was located to the right of the theatre for many years. Before the construction of the theatre, the Hahn house was located on the lot. The building was constructed in 1938 for the theatre and back then, ticket prices were 35¢ for adults and 9¢ for children. A 1950 fire damaged the theatre (due to a popcorn popper incident), but it was renovated and reopened. Through the years, the managers have become familiar friends with the townspeople. Jay Beach was the manager there from 1946 until 1974. C.J. Hayes started working there in 1950 and became the manager in the early 1970s. Mr. Hayes and wife Pauline still manage the theatre today for Carmike Cinema and only charge $1.50 for admission, a bargain in today's world. The theatre is a must-see for its unique identity and loyal presence in downtown Boone. (Courtesy C.J. and Pauline Hayes.)

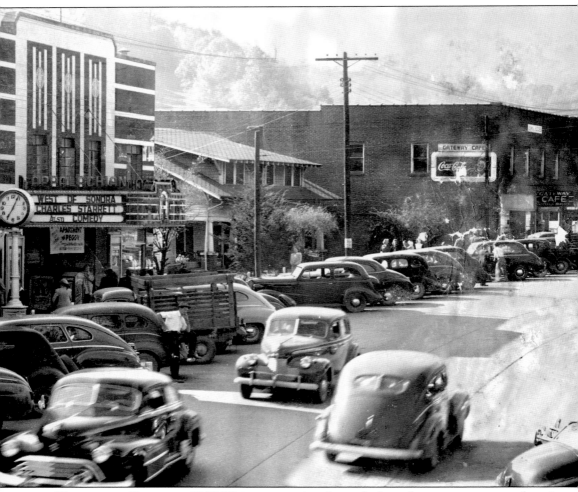

DOWNTOWN BOONE IN 1947. This western view shows the busy downtown area on a shopping day. At the Appalachian Theatre, the movie *West of Sonora* dates the photograph to 1947. The theatre was built in 1938 and is one of the few longtime businesses, along with Boone Drug and Farmer's Hardware, to remain in downtown from these early years. The Green Inn is located next to the theatre, but is now a parking lot. The Gateway Café is next. A bowling alley and pool-room operated in the basement of the Gateway Café. Palmer's Photo Shop, the likely source for many of the older shots used in this book, was located next to the Gateway Café. Palmer Blair operated the shop in downtown for many years until his untimely death in a plane crash. (Courtesy University Archives and Records, Appalachian State University.)

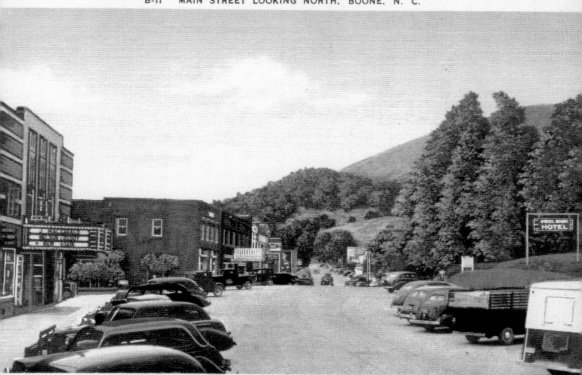

E-9475

MAIN STREET LOOKING NORTH, 1940. This western view of what is now King Street shows the busy downtown marketplace. On the right is the sign for Daniel Boone Hotel. On the left is the Appalachian Theatre with a marquee. The projecting marquee was striking and made of glass. The featured movie here is *J MacDonald, Nelson Eddy, New Moon*. Beside the theatre is likely the Green Inn, retail stores, and the Critcher Hotel with the veranda. At one point, King Street was referred to as Main Street, as on this postcard. Note the early pick-up truck, a predecessor to the modern pickups so common in downtown today. (Courtesy Richard Trexler and Brian Lambeth.)

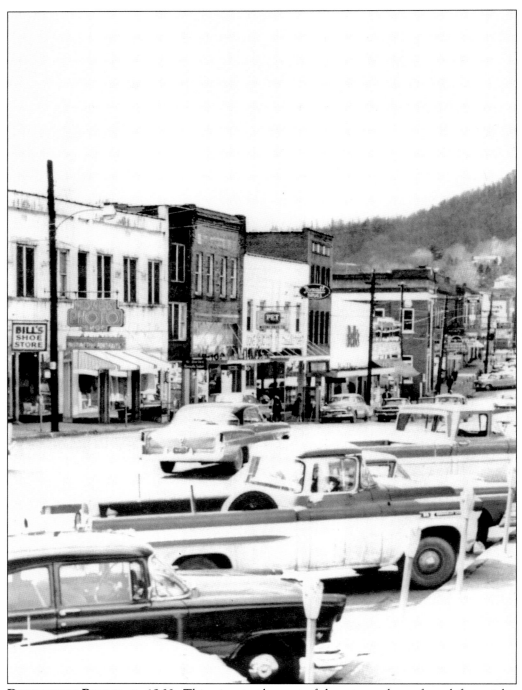

DOWNTOWN BOONE, C. 1960. This view to the east of downtown shows from left to right, Bill's Shoe Store, Flower's Photo, Boone Drug, and Belk's. The Watauga County bank building is on the corner of Depot and King Street. These buildings have been preserved and remain in downtown today. A mix of retail, antiques, and restaurants occupy the buildings. (Courtesy University Archives and Records, Appalachian State University.)

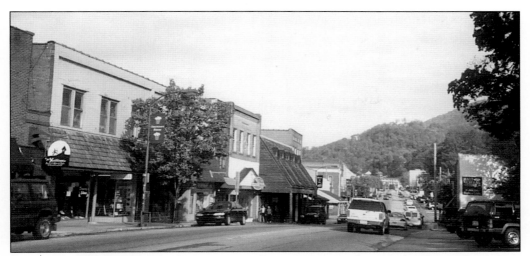

DOWNTOWN BOONE TODAY. This same view of King Street in a photograph taken with a view to the west, bears a slight resemblance to the previous downtown scenes. Several buildings remain from the past, but the older hotels have been long gone. Farmer's Hardware, still a thriving and fascinating store, now occupies the corner building previously occupied by Watauga Bank. The Mast Store now is located in the Hunt Department store building and offers unique clothes and gifts. As can be seen, downtown remains a busy place with plenty of traffic and shopping. Although many downtowns have suffered with the advent of shopping malls, strip centers, and megastores, Boone has managed to offer a variety of goods and services that appeal to locals, college students, and tourists as well. In fact, it's usually a challenge to locate parking in this bustling area. (Courtesy Donna Warmuth.)

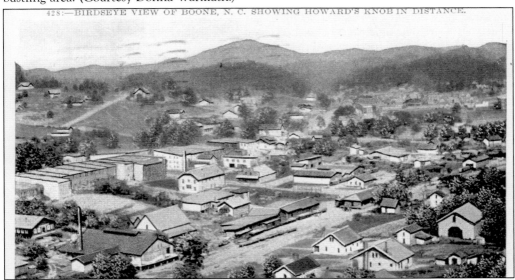

BIRD'S EYE VIEW OF BOONE. This postcard is postmarked 1928 and is an eastern view of downtown and the railroad area and later Rivers Street. The white bungalow in the bottom right corner still sits south of Rivers Street beside the Appalachian State University campus. The long building with a smokestack may have been a railway warehouse. Train cars appear to be lined up in the middle of the photograph. The rear of the commercial buildings on King Street is on the left of the card. (Courtesy Brian Lambeth.)

29

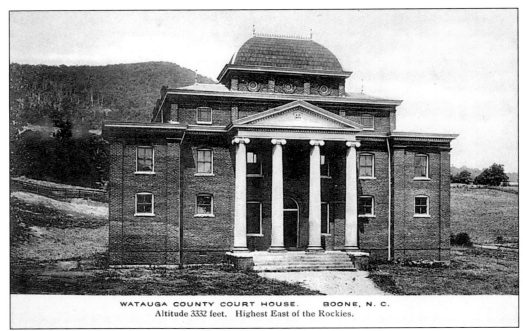

WATAUGA COUNTY COURT HOUSE.   BOONE, N. C.
Altitude 3332 feet.   Highest East of the Rockies.

WATAUGA COUNTY COURTHOUSE C. 1930. Constructed in 1904, this building was the third courthouse for Boone. The shingled tower and white columns added to its attractive appearance. Old-timers recall horse-trading taking place behind the courthouse. The first courthouse, which stood on the hill where the Linney and Moretz houses were located, was built in 1850 on land donated by Jordan Councill Jr. and Ransom Hayes. This courthouse was burned along with the town records in 1873. In 1875, the lot at the corner of King and Water Streets was purchased and a new courthouse was built for $4,800. This 1875 courthouse was replaced by the courthouse shown in this 1904 photograph. In 1967, this beautiful courthouse was demolished to build the present modern courthouse. Many Boone citizens still mourn the loss of this lovely structure with its stately architecture and commanding presence. (Courtesy North Carolina Museum of History and Watauga County Public Library.)

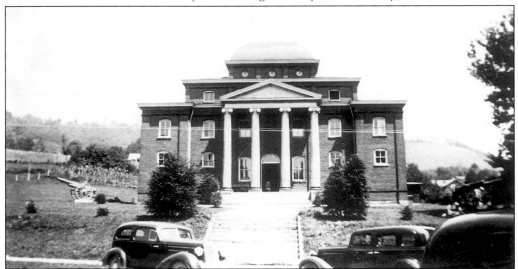

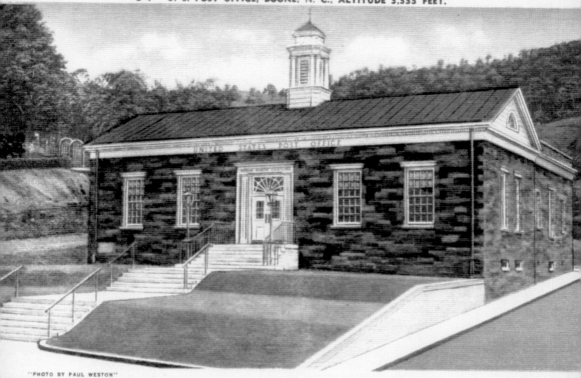

"PHOTO BY PAUL WESTON"

UNITED STATES POST OFFICE, BOONE. The downtown post office in Boone was built in 1938 and has been listed on the National Register of Historic Places. Council's store was the first post office, also at this site. Inside the building is a beautiful mural, created by Alan Tompkins, showing Daniel Boone (in the felt hat, not the recounted coonskin cap) and fellow long hunters on a hunting trip. The natural rock exterior and simple design fits well in the mountains here. The morning trip to check the post office box, complete with greeting old friends, is an important ritual here today as in the past.(Courtesy Brian Lambeth.)

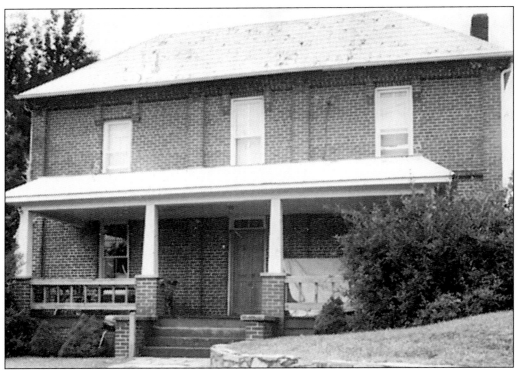

THE JAILHOUSE. One of the oldest remaining buildings in Boone, the jailhouse building has stood on Water Street since 1889. William Stephenson of Mayesville, Kentucky constructed the jail for a cost of $5,000. This building is the fourth jail for the town. Reportedly, a whipping post was once located behind the building. One interesting feature of the building is that the outside walls are 12 inches thick. The jailer used the two front rooms downstairs and upstairs as living area. An iron cage in the center of the room was used for criminal prisoners. Since 1925, the building has been used as a home and for apartments. (Courtesy Historic Boone.)

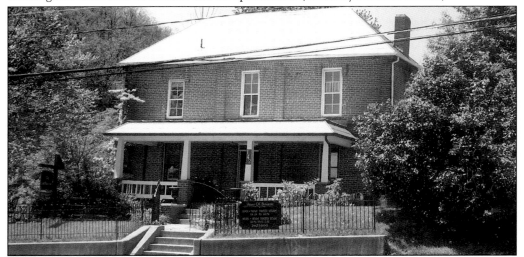

THE JAILHOUSE TODAY. After suffering wear and tear as a rental unit, the jailhouse now houses an elegant Indian restaurant, aptly named The Jailhouse. (Courtesy Donna Warmuth.)

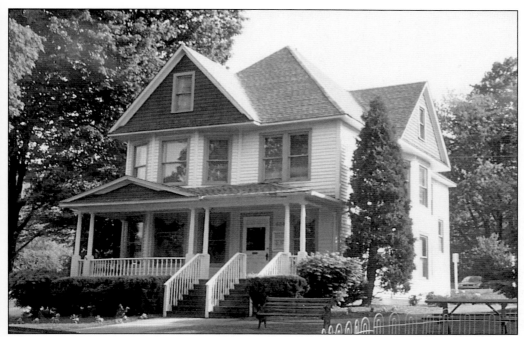

JONES HOUSE. This beautiful Victorian house is located in downtown Boone beside the Mast Store. It was built by Dr. John Walter Jones, an early town physician, in 1908. In 1982, the house was bought by the town of Boone to create a community center. The Watauga County Arts Council has offices in the building and offers exhibit space inside. With its lush lawn, the lot provides one of the few green spaces in downtown Boone. (Courtesy Donna Warmuth.)

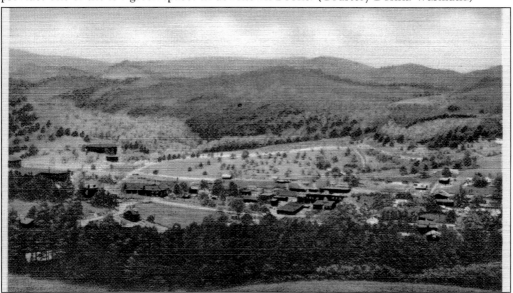

PANORAMIC VIEW OF BOONE. This postcard, probably dating to the 1930s or 1940s, shows a view of Boone from Howard's Knob. Few buildings can be recognized, but the image provides a view of the development that had already taken place in this narrow valley. (Courtesy Brian Lambeth.)

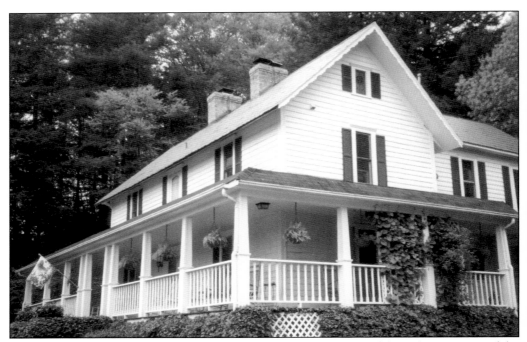

LOVILL HOUSE. Now a lovely bed and breakfast, this well-maintained frame house is one of the older buildings in town. The house was built in 1875 by Capt. E.F. Lovill, a Civil War hero and state senator. (Courtesy Donna Warmuth.)

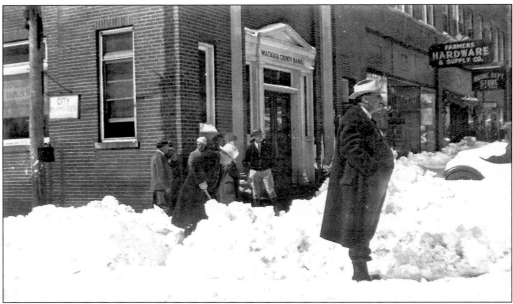

MAYOR WATT GRAGG AND PEDESTRIANS. Mayor Gragg, identified as the man in the foreground, seems undecided about crossing a snowy King Street. The Watauga County Bank, which is now Farmer's Hardware, can be seen on the corner of King and Depot Streets. Farmers Hardware is next to the bank, followed by the Boone Department Store. (Courtesy Historic Boone.)

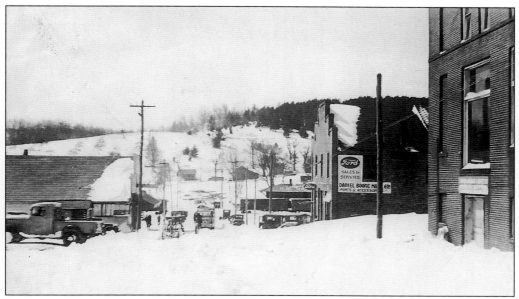

DEPOT STREET IN THE SNOW, 1920s. This southern view of Depot Street illustrates the deep snows of the past that the "old timers" here still talk about. The Daniel Boone Motor Company was located in the brick building on the right. This building would later be used for town offices. Train cars on the railroad tracks can be seen next to it. (Courtesy Historic Boone.)

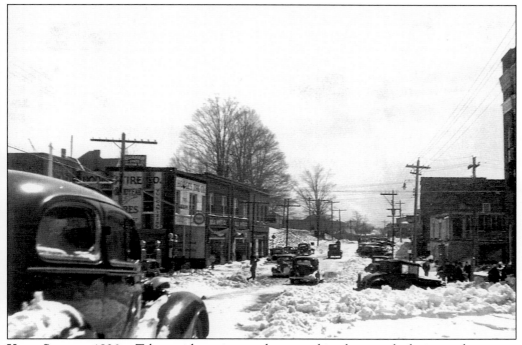

KING STREET, 1930s. Taken with a view to the east, this photograph depicts a deep snow downtown. On the right, the Farmer's Hardware sign is visible. Hodges Tire Co. can be seen on the left at the corner of Depot and King Streets. (Courtesy Historic Boone.)

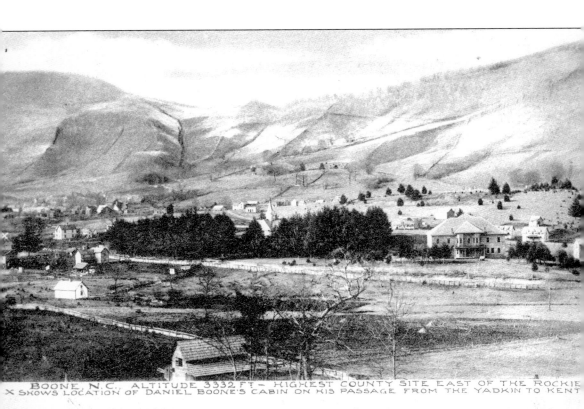

BOONE, N.C., ALTITUDE 3332 FT – HIGHEST COUNTY SITE EAST OF THE ROCKIE
X SHOWS LOCATION OF DANIEL BOONE'S CABIN ON HIS PASSAGE FROM THE YADKIN TO KENT

BOONE, NORTH CAROLINA, ALTITUDE 3,332 FEET. This postcard is a northern view toward Howard's Knob looking at the town. The image shows the steep slopes which were cleared and logged in the early 1900s. With its steeple, Watauga Academy rises from the trees in the center of the photograph. The Administration Building for Appalachian Training School is the large building with a hipped roof to the right of the image, and the Lovill house is to the right of that. Due to the absence of Science Hall, which was built in 1911, it is possible to date the postcard between 1905 and 1911. The "X" on the far left of the image marks the location of the Howard cabin that Daniel Boone used. Agricultural fields with conical hay stacks in the foreground and farmhouses reflect the once-rural atmosphere of this mountain town. The close physical relationship between the town and college has been essential in establishing cooperation between the two groups. (Courtesy Anna Boyce Phillips.)

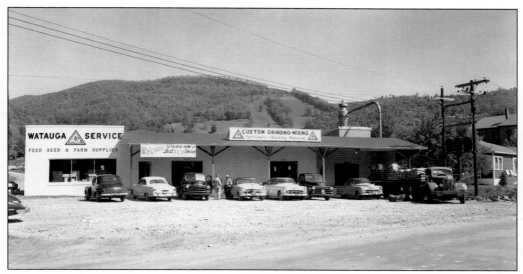

WATAUGA FEED SEED AND FARM SUPPLIES/FCX 1955. This business provided agricultural and garden supplies to the Boone population as well as county residents. Southern States Co-op is now located in the same building on the corner of Water and Rivers Streets. Southern States provides the same necessary supplies for professional and amateur farmers in the area. (Courtesy George Flowers and Boone Chamber of Commerce.)

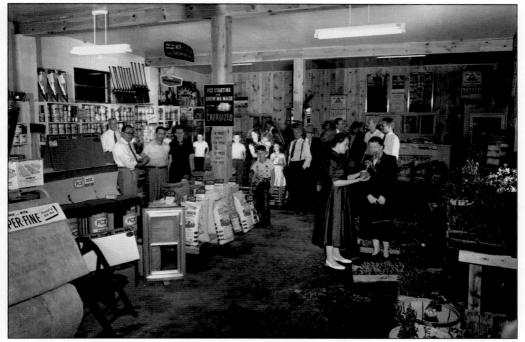

INTERIOR OF WATAUGA FEED, SEED AND FARM SUPPLIES. The interior of Watauga Feed, Seed and Farm Supplies/FCX was a busy place. The ladies, dressed up for a trip to town, are examining plants while the other shoppers appear to be posing for the camera. Now Southern States, the store still serves as a place to meet, greet, and visit. (Courtesy George Flowers and Boone Chamber of Commerce.)

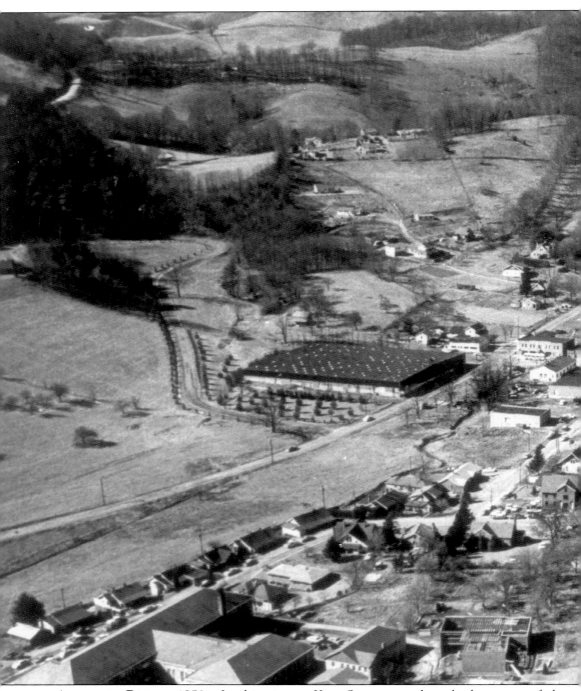

AERIAL OF BOONE, 1950S. In this picture, King Street runs through the center of the photograph. Whitener Hall (ASU) and Boone Baptist Church are visible on the lower left. Just above that, the building with the domed sanctuary is the Boone United Methodist Church. The Daniel Boone Hotel, the large multistory building, is standing just to the right of King Street in the center. Part of the campus of Appalachian State University is located along the

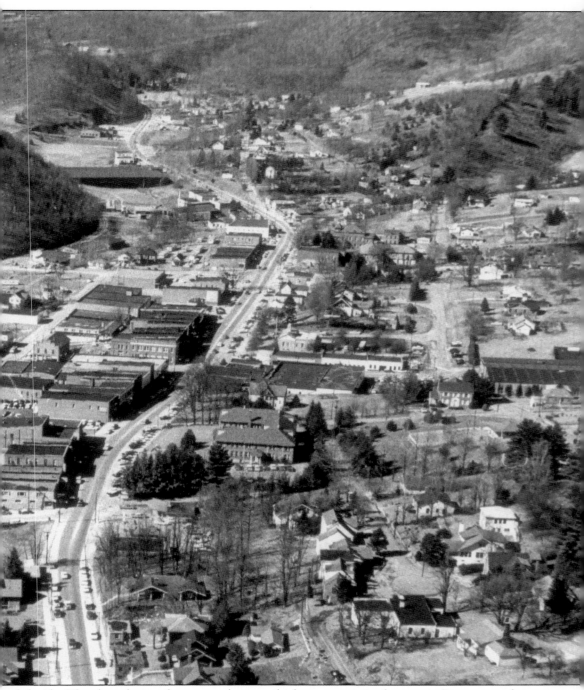

left side. The three large tobacco warehouses which were once in downtown Boone can also be seen. Many of the downtown buildings shown here are still present and in use. The low density residential neighborhoods on the right of the photograph contrast with the higher density commercial areas of downtown. The mature trees add to the "green appeal" of the town. (Courtesy Historic Boone.)

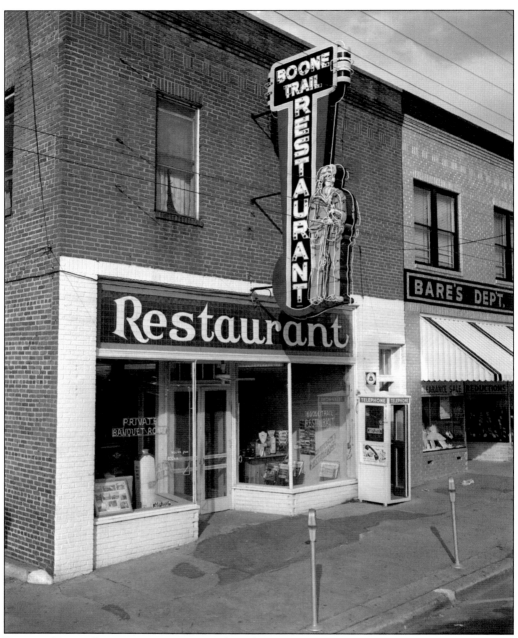

BOONE TRAIL RESTAURANT, 1956. This photograph shows the Boone Trail Restaurant, which was located on the south side of King Street along the Farmer's Hardware block. Bare's Department Store was located next door. The restaurant obviously was promoting the Daniel Boone image of the town with the "life sized" Boone figure on the sign. (Courtesy George Flowers and Boone Chamber of Commerce.)

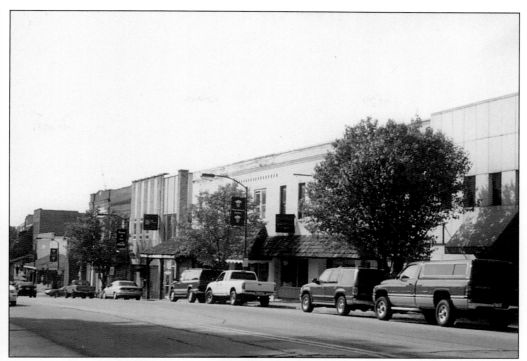

FARMER'S HARDWARE BLOCK TODAY. This photograph is a view of the same area of King Street as shown in the previous photographs. For the most part, the integrity of the architecture of the old buildings has been maintained, although some buildings have modern facades. The uses here range from banks to retail to office spaces. (Courtesy Donna Warmuth.)

CHRISTMAS DAY FIRE 1952. This fire was estimated by newspapers to be the most devastating in the history of Boone. The fire destroyed the Qualls block of buildings. Since electricity was cut off, many Boone residents had a cold Christmas dinner by candlelight. The Skyline Café (long a gathering place downtown), the Carolina Hotel (the town's second largest hotel), and the City Meat Market were all lost to the fire. The losses were estimated to be $167,000. (Courtesy George Flowers and Boone Chamber of Commerce.)

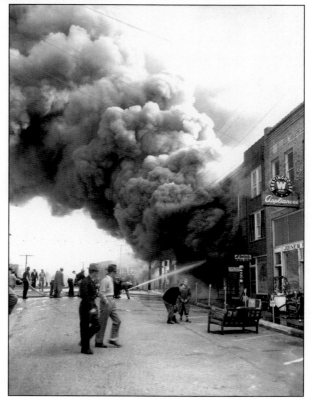

41

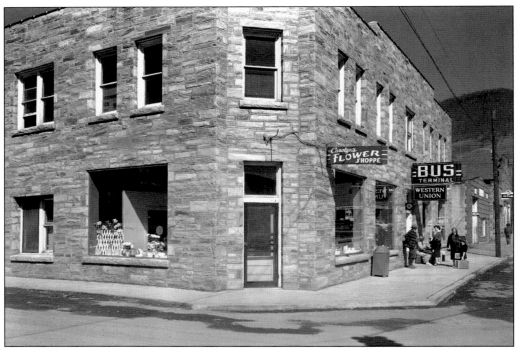

GREYHOUND BUS STATION. The location of this bus station is how Depot Street received its name. The bus connection of Boone to other cities was key in opening it up for residents, visitors, and tourists. Caroline's Flower Shop was also located in the building. The stone building is still located here and belongs to a church. This area was once a gathering place in downtown. (Courtesy George Flowers and Boone Chamber of Commerce.)

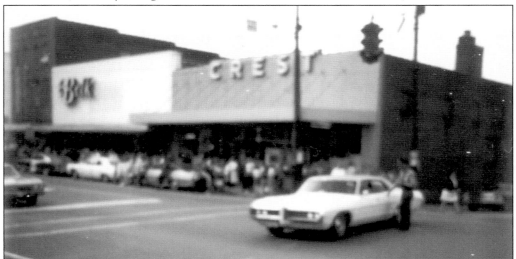

CREST DIMESTORE AND BELK, C. 1970. The Crest Dimestore and Belk store are shown on the south side of King Street. Before strips and shopping malls, these downtown businesses provided the residents with essential items. Many locals remember looking forward to a trip to the Dimestore and Boone Drug soda shop on Saturdays. The buildings still remain and serve various retail uses. (Courtesy Brenda Jones Gragg.)

Two

CHURCHES

Settlers soon needed churches in these rugged mountains. Although first served by circuit-riding ministers, religious groups later met in homes, often only one Sunday a month because of the difficulty of travel. Most of the settlers were Protestant and originally Presbyterian. However, the populace soon changed to other denominations, because they were too independent for Calvinism.

Three Forks Baptist Church, the earliest organized denomination in Watauga County, was organized in 1790. The first church in Boone was the Boone Methodist Church, organized in 1866. Other early churches include First Baptist Church, Advent Christian Church, Saint Luke's Episcopal Church, Grace Evangelical Lutheran Church, Boone Methodist Church, Mennonite Brethren Church, First Presbyterian Church, Perkinsville Baptist Church, and St. Elizabeth Catholic Church

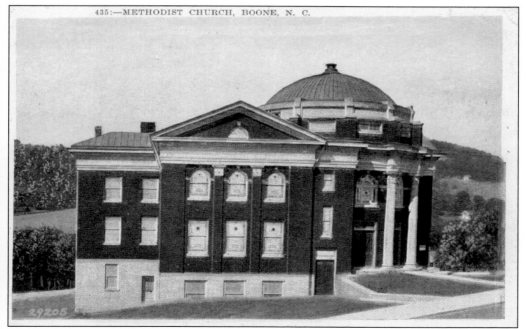

BOONE METHODIST CHURCH. This postcard was sent in 1946 and shows a side view of the lovely design and rotunda of the Boone United Methodist Church. This church building was completed in 1926, although two church buildings at different locations preceded it. (Courtesy Brian Lambeth.)

43

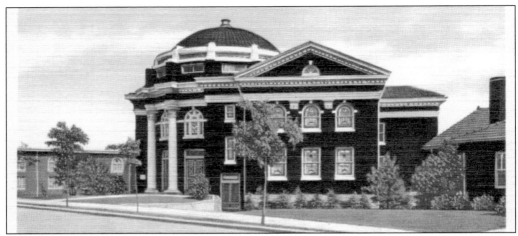

FIRST METHODIST CHURCH. This church building was built in 1925 on King Street. It was the first church in Boone, organized in 1866. The Methodists have built and occupied four different churches on different sites since 1873. The sanctuary shown on this card was finished in 1925 at a new site on E. King Street. Families who were active in the early church included Bingham, Blair, Blackburn, Councill, Critcher, Hardin, Linney, Lovill, Norris, and Rivers. (Courtesy Brian Lambeth.)

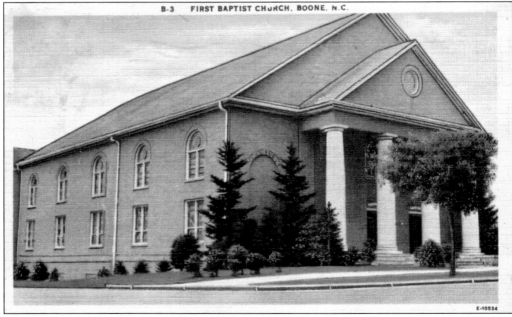

FIRST BAPTIST CHURCH C. 1950. Organized in 1885, the first building for the Boone Baptist Church congregation was located on Rivers Street. The sanctuary of the handsome brick building was built in 1937, and the chapel was added in 1965. Families involved in the early history of the church include the Critcher, Coffey, Gragg, Bryan, Greer, Holtzclaw, and Hall families. This postcard, postmarked 1954, is addressed to Mrs. Ira Pearson from the Buchanans. It reads, "Attended S.S. & Church here this morning. I visited the opening of the Primary Dept. It was nice but had nothing on ours. Are enjoying our stay here. Love to you & yours, also the entire church." (Courtesy Richard Trexler and Brian Lambeth.)

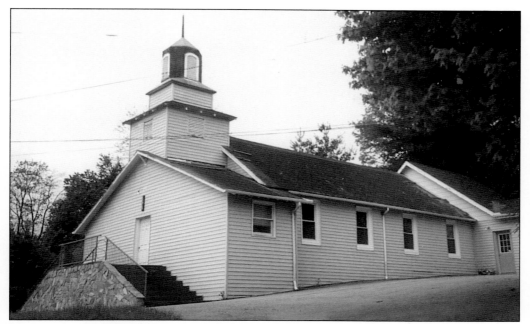

MENNONITE BRETHREN CHURCH. The congregation for this church first met in 1912 and this building was constructed in the Junaluska community just north of downtown in 1917. Mennonite missionaries had visited nearby Elk Park and decided to form a church in Boone. The primarily African-American community in the Junaluska neighborhood has developed their own unique type of Mennonite faith, and the church and its respected ministers continue to play a strong role in the community. The Junaluska community is the last intact historic neighborhood left in town. (Courtesy Donna Warmuth.)

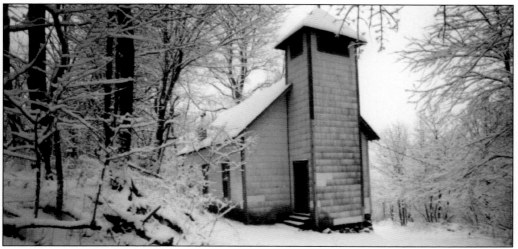

BOONE METHODIST CHAPEL. Built in 1898, this church was previously located in the Junaluska community and used to be the oldest black church in the county. The church flourished in the early 1900s and with the later Mennonite Church, served as a religious and social center for the community. The building also served as a community school in the early 1900s. Unfortunately, the church was closed in 1989 and was demolished by a landowner in 1996. (Courtesy Junaluska Heritage Foundation.)

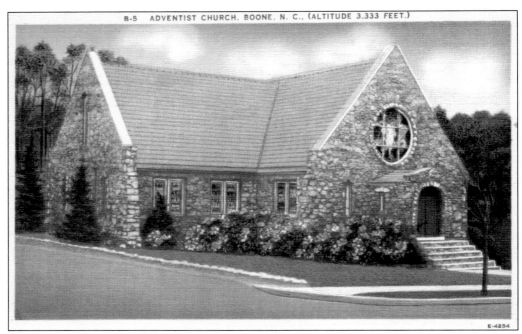

B-5 ADVENTIST CHURCH. BOONE. N. C., (ALTITUDE 3.333 FEET.)

ADVENT CHRISTIAN CHURCH. The Adventist Church, surrounded by colorful pink rhododendrons, is located on the eastern end of King Street and was completed in 1926. The stone construction adds to its aesthetic appeal. (Courtesy Brian Lambeth.)

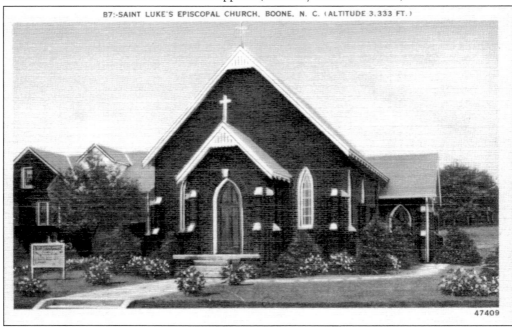

B7:-SAINT LUKE'S EPISCOPAL CHURCH. BOONE. N. C. (ALTITUDE 3.333 FT.)

SAINT LUKE'S EPISCOPAL CHURCH. This brick church was built on College Street in 1940. It has Gothic features, including the arched windows and door. Originally next to the campus of Appalachian State University, it was preserved and recently moved to the site of the new Saint Luke's Church north of King Street on the east end of downtown. (Courtesy Brian Lambeth.)

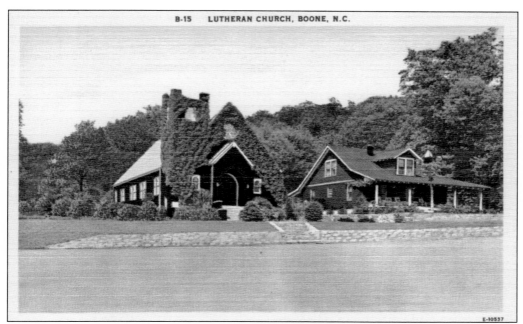

GRACE EVANGELICAL LUTHERAN CHURCH. This handsome brick church adorned in ivy is located on the east end of King Street. The first church was built in 1928 and the newer addition was constructed in 1987. The attractive brick bungalow is no longer there. (Courtesy Brian Lambeth.)

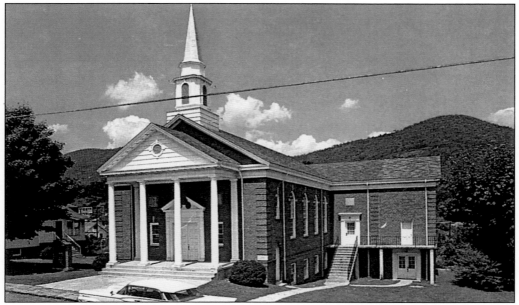

FIRST PRESBYTERIAN CHURCH IN 1963. This postcard shows the stately brick First Presbyterian Church located opposite the Appalachian State University campus. The First Presbyterian Church in Boone was founded in 1939 and first met in the old Appalachian High School building. This church was built on the site in 1941 and has been added onto over time. (Courtesy Historic Boone.)

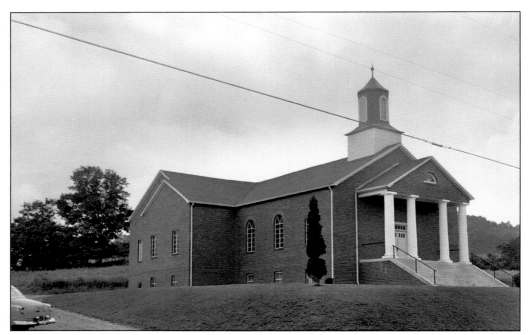

PERKINSVILLE BAPTIST CHURCH 1957. Located on Highway 194, this church was organized in 1947, and the current church was built in 1949. (Courtesy George Flowers and Boone Chamber of Commerce.)

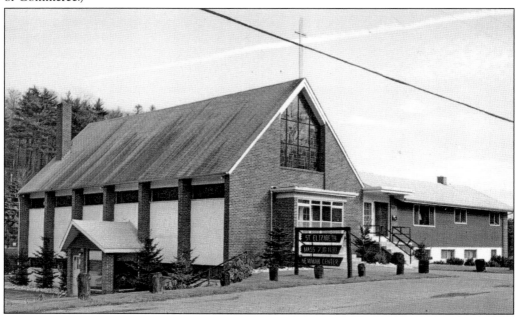

ST. ELIZABETH CATHOLIC CHURCH C. 1970. This Catholic Church was built in 1958 on U.S. Highway 321, at the current location of Blockbuster Video. By 1984, a fire had destroyed the building on the postcard, and a new larger church was finished in 1988 on Pilgrims Way. The remaining side addition on the original church was moved across Faculty Street and now houses the Catholic Campus Ministry. (Courtesy St. Elizabeth Catholic Church.)

Three

PARADES, SOCIALIZING, AND SUNDRY CELEBRATIONS

Boone has always been a community of clubs, festivals, and celebrations. Folks here just seem to like to get together and share thoughts, opinions, and fun with family or strangers. The first settlers were brave souls and all those who have followed have added to this thriving, diverse community.

Early social life centered around churches and schools but soon expanded to various social clubs. Traditional social occasions such as quilting bees and barn raisings were common in the past, and the functions of these meetings transitioned into social clubs. Community pride and sharing that pride with tourists has been a source of enjoyment for many. Still today, festivals abound in the High Country, from the Wooly Worm Festival to Art in the Park in Blowing Rock.

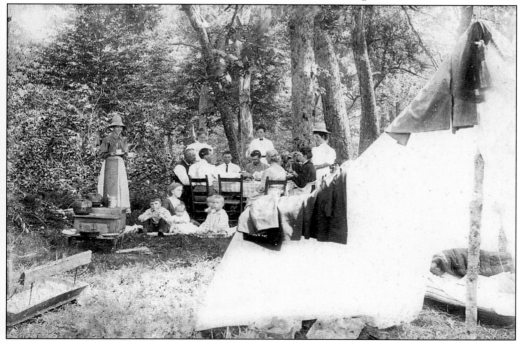

CAMPING C. 1900. Folks have always been interested in exploring the great outdoors, even when everyday life would have been considered roughing it for most of us today. The tent has been set up, and the stove is keeping lunch warm for these Victorian campers in the area. Attractive campgrounds still are abundant in the area, especially along the Blue Ridge Parkway. (Courtesy Historic Boone.)

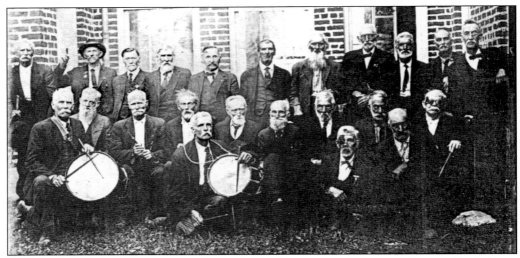

WATAUGA COUNTY CONFEDERATE VETERANS. This reunion of Watauga County Confederate Veterans appears to date from about 1910. Watauga County supplied many soldiers to the Confederate army, but some also joined the Union ranks. Pictured from left to right are (front row) two unidentified, Ranzy Miller, unidentified, Wiley Norris, unidentified, Wyatt Hayes, Henry Harrison Farthing, Calvin Cottrell, unidentified, Webster Davis, and Speck Hanson; (back row) unidentified, Elijah Norris, William Blair, unidentified, ? Critcher, John Hodges, Harvey Davis, Capt. Bill Hodges, unidentified, Jerome Presnell, and Bill Norris. (Courtesy Historic Boone.)

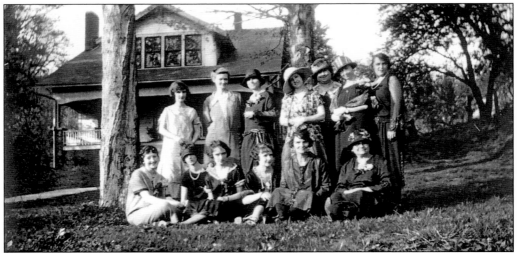

THE FRIDAY AFTERNOON CLUB C. 1925. This group was formed in 1918 as a social and needlework club. Daughters of members would automatically gain an invitation to join. The photograph was taken in front of the home of MaeBelle and Austin Enoch South on North Water Street. Pictured from left to right are (front row) Grace McNinch Council (Mrs. Tracy Council), Mrs. Dean Bingham, Lucy Greene (Mrs. David Greene), Mae Johnson, "Bessie" Casey (Mrs. W.T. Casey), and Mrs. R.M. Greene (sister of Dr. D.D. and B.B. Dougherty, founders of Appalachian State University); (back row) Mrs. Woosley (the Methodist Minister's wife), Mrs. J.D. Rankin, Mrs. Will Winkler, Mrs. Sproles, Mrs. Frank Linney, Miss Annie Stanberry (later Mrs. R.L. Clay), and Mrs. Jennie Critcher. (Courtesy Historic Boone.)

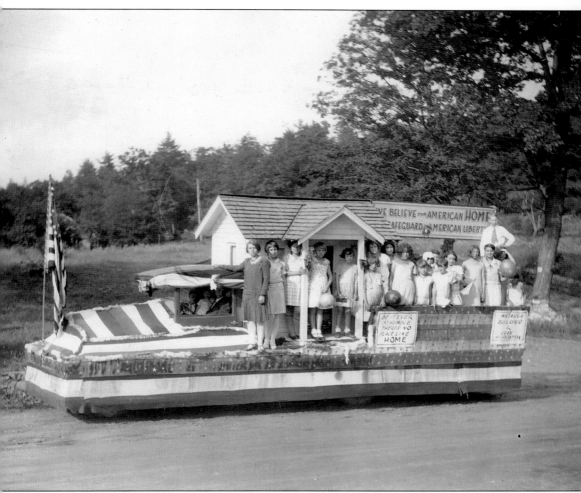

FOURTH OF JULY PARADE, 1930s. This patriotic float, by Watauga Building and Loan Association, is symbolic of the intense hometown pride for which Boone is known. Competition to design the best parade floats continues to be quite fierce. This mortgage bank was located on King Street near the intersection with Depot Street. In this time period, home ownership was being promoted The sign on the float reads "We believe the American home can safeguard American liberty." (Courtesy Historic Boone.)

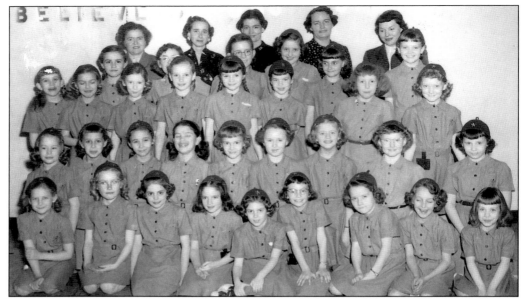

BROWNIE TROOP IN THE 1950S. This delightful group of Brownie Scouts is, from left to right: (first row) Sara Lou Haggaman, unidentified, Gloria Storie, Ruth Ann Williams, Leslie Hardin, Kathryn Kelly, unidentified, and Linda Lyon; (second row) unidentified, Maria Erneston, Carol Lee Critcher, Patty Sue Spencer, Sylvia Crew, Carol Congleton, Lenore Nash, unidentified, and Mackie Haggaman; (third row) three unidentified girls, Pam Haggaman, two unidentified girls, and Linda Lackey; (fourth row) Jamie Price, unidentified, Nancy Pease, Janie Buchland, Barbara Mast, and two unidentified girls; (fifth row) Jay Lou Carpenter, Carolyn Winkler Congleton, unidentified, Elsie Erneston (?), and unidentified. (Courtesy Historic Boone.)

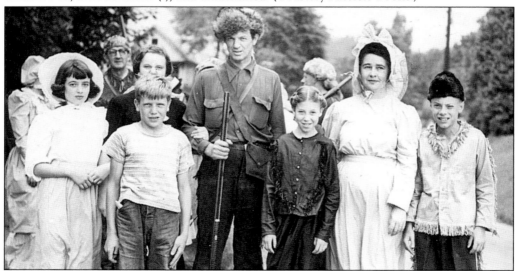

BOONE 1949 CENTENNIAL CELEBRATION. In 1949, Watauga County celebrated its 100th birthday in high style with a historical pageant, *Echoes of the Blue Ridge*. Hundreds of town and county residents participated in this community event. The play was staged and produced by Pat Alderman. Pictured from left to right are Bette Swain Gabriel, Grady Farthing, Ann Cottrell, Kent Brown, Louise de Lima, and Mark Hodges. (Courtesy Historic Boone.)

WATAUGA COUNTY CENTENNIAL, 1949. Earl "Jerry" Coe, former mayor Watt Gragg, and future mayor Wade Brown are shown participating in the 1949 Centennial celebration. The Boone post office can be seen in the background. (Courtesy Historic Boone.)

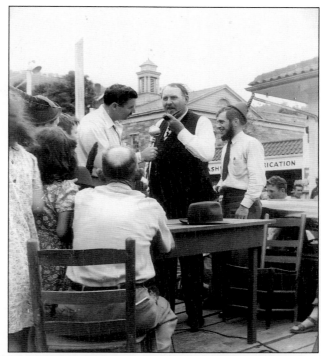

ALL DRESSED UP FOR THE 1949 CENTENNIAL. These folks portrayed different characters in the *Echoes of the Blue Ridge* pageant, produced in July 1949. It was impressive that so many citizens participated in the event. Pictured in this photograph are, from left to right, Ann Carroll, Dr. J.T.C. Wright, Barbara Jones, and Cecil Miller. (Courtesy Historic Boone.)

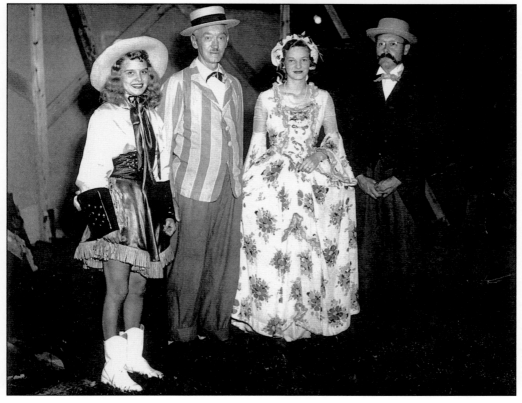

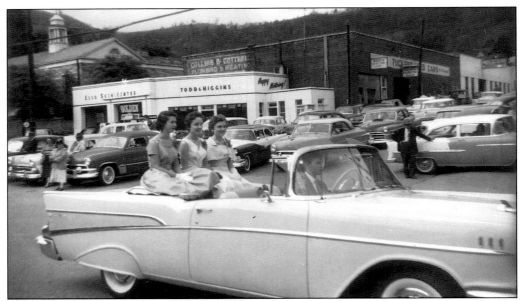

DOWNTOWN A.S.T.C. PARADE, C. 1956. From left to right, riding in the car, are unidentified, Rebecca Bingham Mast, and Joan Cotton. The recently opened Esso Service Station is the white building. Collins & Cotrell Plumbing and Heating and Tuckers Used Cars occupy the buildings in the right of the photograph. (Courtesy Historic Boone.)

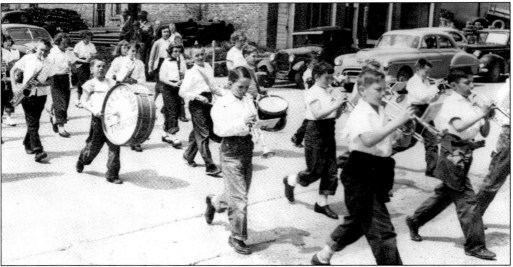

MARCHING ACROSS HOWARD STREET. This parade of the Troubadours of Appalachian Elementary School is crossing the intersection of Howard and Depot Streets in 1952. Behind them, the brick building is the former Boone City Hall, once a Ford dealership, and now a bike shop. The students are identified, from left to right, as (first row) Frank Payne Jr. and Tommy Owsley; (second row) Gary Mast, unidentified, and Bob Agle Jr.; (third row) Richard Agle, Bob Cook, and Bobby Joe Winkler; (fourth row) Tad Buckland, Jim Goodnight, an unidentified saxophonist, Margaret Rose Brown, and unidentified; (fifth row) Pat Maddox and Libby Culbreth; (sixth row) Gloria Hampton and unidentified. (Courtesy Historic Boone; photograph by Palmer Blair.)

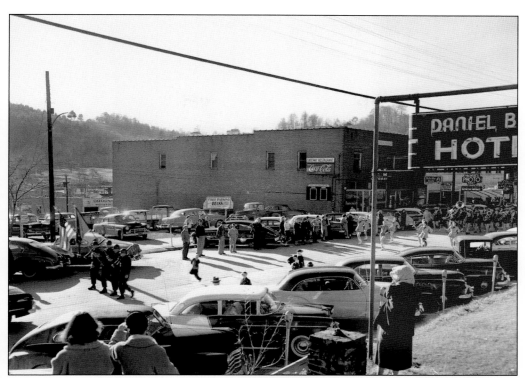

AMERICAN LEGION PARADE OCTOBER 1955. Boone has always been very patriotic and has provided many members to the armed services. The Daniel Boone Hotel sign can be seen on the right of the image. Along the south side of King Street, near the intersection of Depot Street, are the following businesses: (from left to right) Gateway Restaurant, Moretz and Sons, Bill's Shoe Store, Palmer Photo, and the Meat Market Grocery. (Courtesy George Flowers and Boone Chamber of Commerce.)

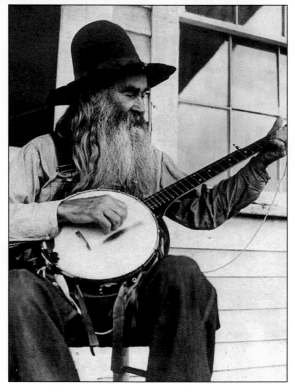

BANJO MAN IN THE EARLY 1950s. This old-timer was photographed by Palmer Blair, an early Boone photographer who had an office on King Street. Traditional music is commonly played in these mountains and the area continues to be home to many famous traditional musicians and instrument craftsmen. (Courtesy Historic Boone.)

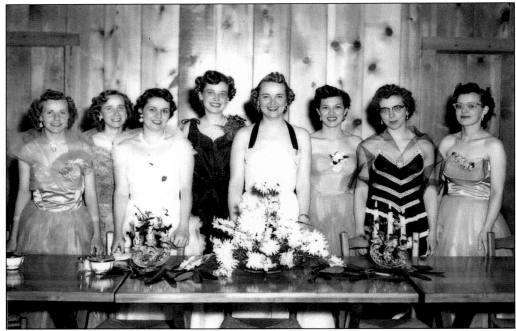

BOONE JUNIOR WOMAN'S CLUB, 1957. This group was very active in the Boone community. In this time period, ladies really "put on the dog" when attending club meetings. Pictured from left to right are Marbeth (Winkler) Fiddler, Carolyn (Winkler) Congleton, Elsie Erneston, Mary Lou Craven, Lib (South) Storie, Ina Spencer, Bettye Davis, and Carrie Lee Dickerson. (Courtesy Historic Boone.)

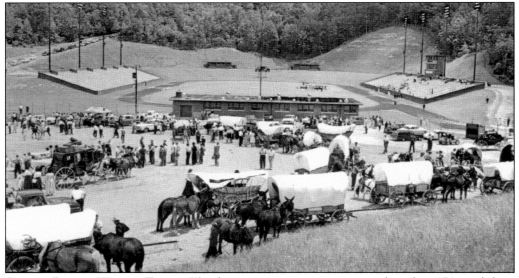

DANIEL BOONE WAGON TRAIN. The famous wagon train was started in the 1970s and drew many spectators on its route down King Street and along parts of the old Buffalo Trail. The card reads, "Terminating at the stadium on the campus of Appalachian State Teachers College, the historic Daniel Boone Wagon Trail was restaged as part of the 300th birthday of the Carolina Charter." (Courtesy Richard Trexler.)

Four

TRANSPORTATION

Although the remote location of Boone is part of its attraction, residents quickly realized that ways of ingress and egress were invaluable to education, trade, and commerce. However, the topography provided a harsh physical barrier that wouldn't be conquered by engineered highways until much later. Horses were used for transportation much longer here than in other parts of the state because of the difficult terrain and road conditions. Through the efforts of Dr. B.B. Dougherty (one of the founders of Watauga Academy), in 1921, a gravel and stone road was built to join Boone to Wilkesboro. This major artery, the "Boone Trail Highway," was paved by 1931 and joined Yadkinville to Tennessee.

Floods in 1916 destroyed a new roadbed linking Boone and Wilkesboro and Lenoir. The Eastern Tennessee and Western North Carolina Railroad track, which ran between the campus and the Dougherty home was all but destroyed by the devastating flood of 1940. Most recently, a section of U.S. Highway 321 near Blowing Rock was temporarily closed because of flooding damage. Due to the road improvements, tourists, second homeowners, and college students have been able to easily access the amenities of Boone. The economy in the high country has benefited from their sojourns here.

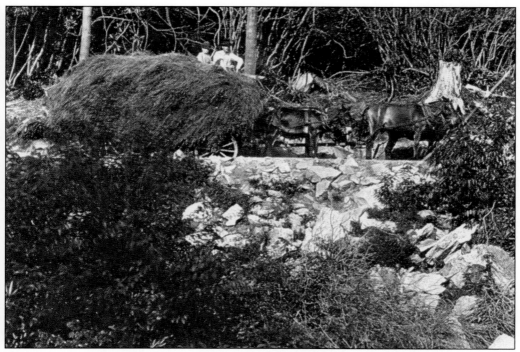

WAGONS ALONG THE TURNPIKE. This 1888 photograph shows the challenges involved in traveling through these mountains. The wagons are traveling along the Blowing Rock Boone Turnpike, still a steep grade today. (Courtesy *The Blowing Rocket*.)

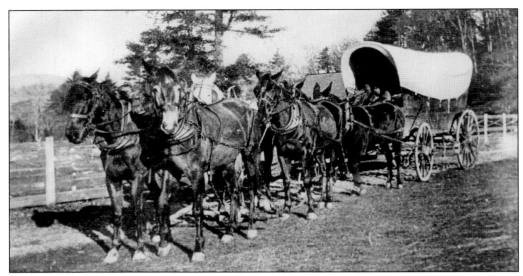

TRANSPORTING GOODS BY HORSE AND WAGON. This schooner, or crooked-bed-type wagon, and a team of horses of the Blair family made it possible to transport goods down the mountain. The schooner wagon was used until about 1910 when farmers changed to using the flat bed or box-bed wagon. According to a Blair family member, wagons hitched to two to six horses would transport wagonloads of cabbage, potatoes, apples, chestnuts, dried fruit, dried beef hams, and port to far away places such as Chester, South Carolina, as well as Hickory, Morganton, Statesville, Charlotte, and Gastonia in North Carolina. The longer trips could take as long as two weeks to complete. (Courtesy Sarah Blair Spencer.)

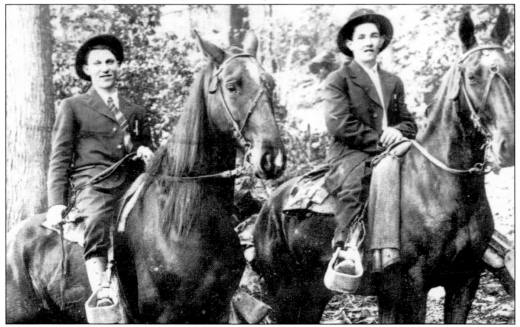

TWO BOYS WENT A-COURTIN.' Partee W. Palmer and Dayton Greene are shown around 1900 going courting on horseback. Even after the introduction of the automobile, travel by horse remained a dependable mode of transportation in this steep terrain. (Courtesy Historic Boone.)

PLANK ROAD NEAR SAWMILL. The first roads in the Boone area were dirt roads, but plank roads, constructed of sawed and planed planks, proved more durable. This road near a sawmill in the county shows the first road improvements in the area. (Courtesy Claude Bodenhamer, original by Paul Weston with Boone Photo Shop.)

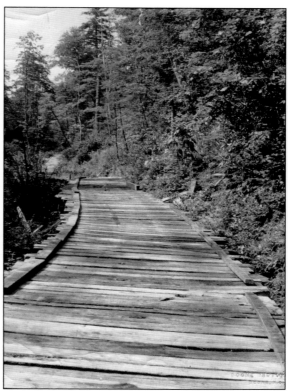

EAST TENNESSEE AND WESTERN NORTH CAROLINA RAILROAD, OCTOBER, 1923. In 1917, this railroad line was installed to Boone. Before that, the closest rail service was in Pineola, 24 miles from Boone. The line later was called Tweetsie for the piercing whistle which echoed through the valley. The 1940 flood destroyed much of the line and operations were discontinued after that. From left to right are C.B. Angel, conductor; Paul Fletcher, brakeman; Ted Blalock, brakeman; Brownie Allison, engineer; and Max Daniels. (Courtesy Historic Boone.)

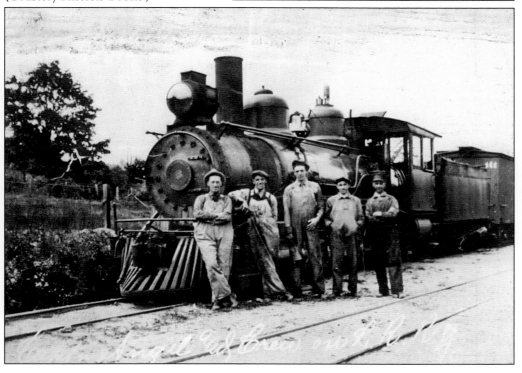

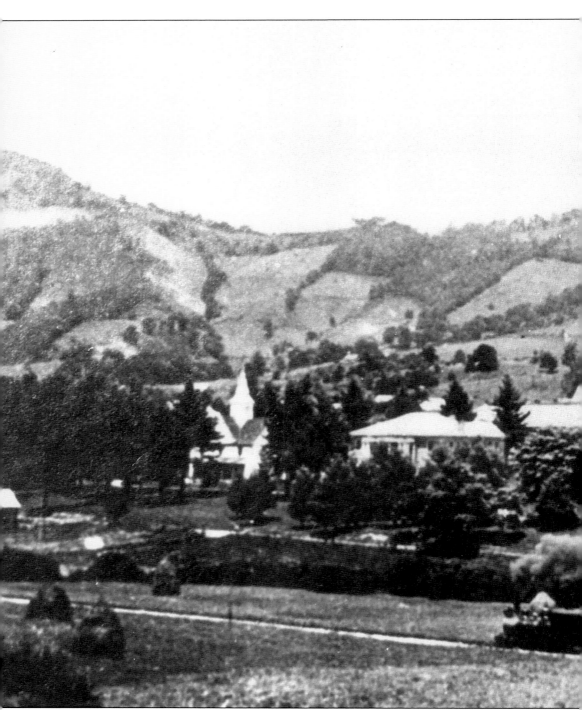

RAILWAY TO BOONE. This c. 1920 photograph shows the East Tennessee and Western North Carolina Railroad line which ran near the campus near the present location of Rivers Street. The train was key in connecting this remote country with larger markets for the exchange of goods. One could ride the train to Johnson City, Tennessee, considered a long trip back then.

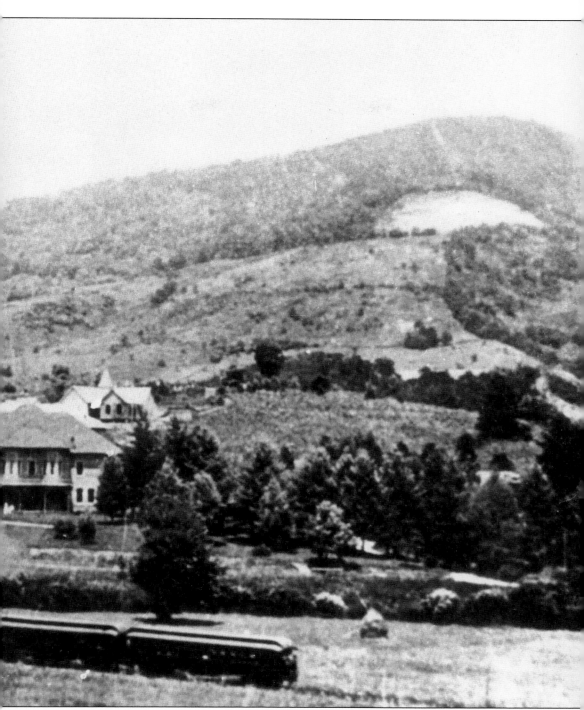

The large building on the right is the first Administration Building and the steepled building is Watauga Academy, on the campus of Appalachian Training School. The hay stacks in the fields illustrate the agricultural heritage of the town. (Courtesy Historic Boone.)

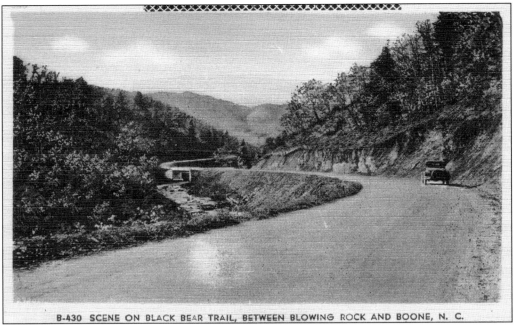

B-430 SCENE ON BLACK BEAR TRAIL, BETWEEN BLOWING ROCK AND BOONE, N. C.

SCENE ON BLACK BEAR TRAIL. This postcard depicts a section of the road between Blowing Rock and Boone. The bar at the top of the postcard indicates it was a salesman's sample card. (Courtesy Brian Lambeth.)

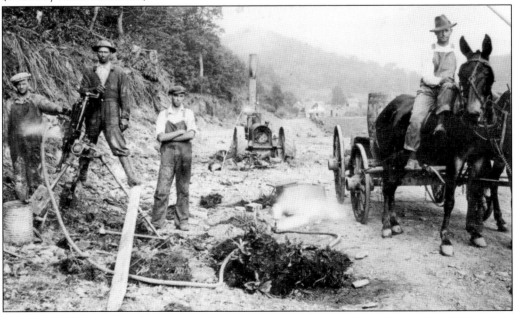

ROAD CONSTRUCTION, MOUNTAIN STYLE. Taken about 1924, this photograph shows the Boone-Blowing Rock road. Zeb Farthing's house can be seen in the center of the background. Pictured in the photograph are (from left to right) Marvin Norris, Grover Norris, Reeves Shores, and Wayne Stout. The steam drill was propelled by the small boiler. (Courtesy Ronald Elrod and *The Blowing Rocket*.)

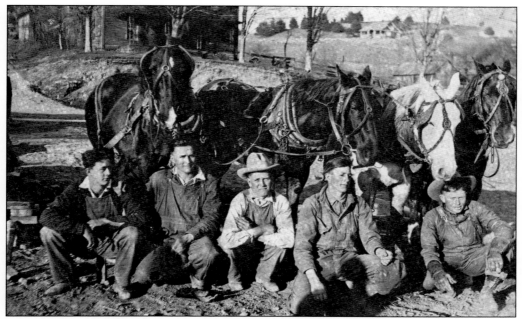

ROAD WORK ON KING STREET. Front left to right, these men are identified as Willard Watson, Clyde Triplett, Ernest Hicks, Jess Laws, and Rob Boone at work on King Street in front of the J.D. "Crack" Council home, which stood at the current site of the downtown post office building. (Courtesy Historic Boone.)

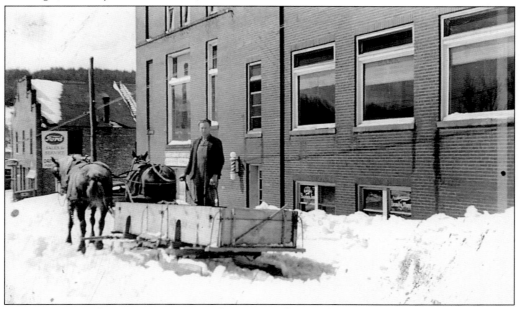

SNOW "HORSE" SLEDDING ON DEPOT STREET. In this southern view along Depot Street, one can see the transportation mode used by many in the snow. The farmer is identified as Earl Blackburn, who often used the horse and sleigh to get around town. The National Barber Shop is in the lower level of the present Farmer's Hardware building and Ford Sales & Service is in the next building. (Courtesy Historic Boone.)

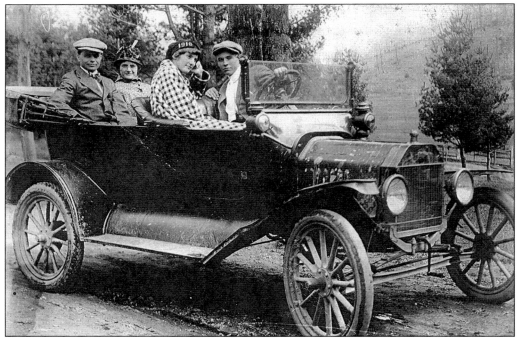

DRIVING IN STYLE IN 1916. The driver is Russell D. Hodges and the front seat passenger is Fay Greer Hodges. The muddy car attests to the state of local roads in that day. They appear to be riding in a 1915 Model T touring car. (Courtesy Historic Boone.)

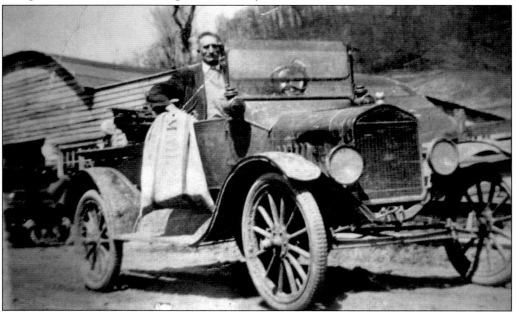

DR. GEORGE H. HAYES IN AN EARLY CAR. Dr. George H. Hayes, the area's first licensed veterinarian, practiced in Boone and Watauga County in the early 1900s. He owned the second automobile in Watauga County. He is shown here proudly posing in his 1916 Model T. (Courtesy Howell Hayes.)

Five

AGRICULTURE AND TRADE

Even with Boone's remote location, it has been a central business center for the immediate region. Councill's Store and the post office in Boone were the mainstays of the area. Market days and horse trading were conducted near the early courthouses, with a liberal dose of politics and gossip. Agriculture was a way of life for most people in Boone and in Watauga County. The soil was fertile and subsistence farmers could forge out a life raising corn, small grains, Irish potatoes, beans, cabbage, livestock, and Burley tobacco. After the train line came through in 1917, goods didn't have to arrive and depart by horse and wagon. Businesses and industry were able to flourish and expand markets as the automobile arrived. The timber of the mountains was discovered in the early 1900s, and the old trees were soon cut down and hauled away. In 1924, one of the early industries in the area was founded, when the North State Canning Company began processing sauerkraut made from local farmers' cabbage. Today, many businesses cater to visitors and college students but have managed to retain a unique mountain flavor.

As the 1925 Directory of Boone proclaimed, "there is no better little town in the state of North Carolina and none, no matter what its size, that has as much 'pep' as has Boone."

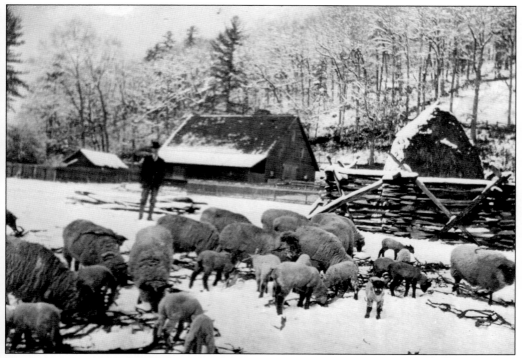

BLAIR FARM. George Henry Blair is pictured about 1890 in front of the barn and shed on the Blair farm. Sheep were well-suited to the cold mountain winters. (Courtesy Historic Boone.)

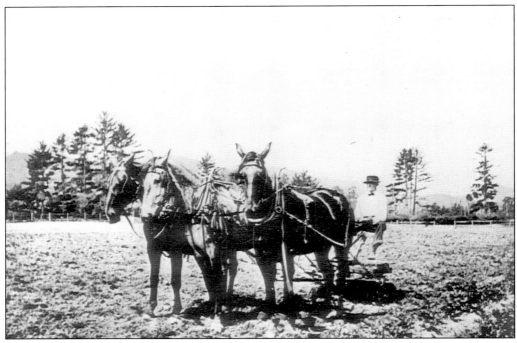

PLOUGHING. Neal Blair sits atop an old plow at the Blair Farm off Deerfield Road. Farming in the days before engines was exhausting and time consuming. The Blair farm covered much of the area of today's Boone Golf Course and the Blair family transported goods by horse and wagon as far away as South Carolina. (Courtesy Sarah Blair Spencer.)

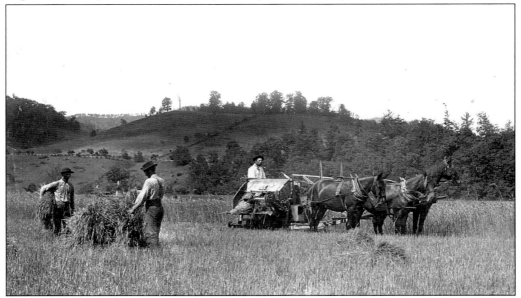

THRESHING SEASON. In this early agricultural scene from the area, a thresher is threshing the wheat while the mules wait patiently. Today, it's almost impossible to make a living from farming, but many people here farm because it's a way of life that runs in their families. (Courtesy Historic Boone.)

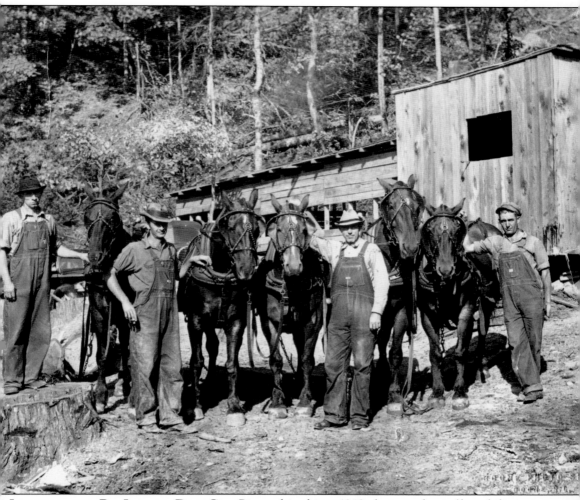

LUMBERING ON BIG LAUREL, DEEP GAP. Pictured in this *c.* 1940 photograph are (from left to right) Leonard Hayes, "Slim" Dobson, Ike Bodenhamer, and Floyd Hicks. Before the modern engine, horses were used to pull large trees from the hillsides and transport them to the sawmills. The work was dangerous and hard but provided jobs to many. The largest lumber operation at Shull's Mill was almost a town onto itself with on-site living quarters, stores, sawmill, and timber plant, owned by Whiting Lumber Company. One of the major reasons for extending the railroad from Johnson City to Boone was to transport the timber to Tennessee. (Courtesy Claude Bodenhamer, original by Paul Weston with Boone Photo Shop.)

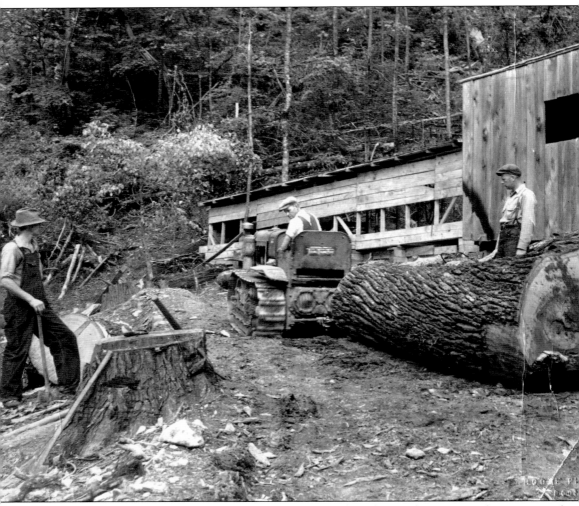

DRAGGING LOGS AT WILEY MARTIN SAWMILL. The advent of engines and tractors made lumbering safer and more efficient as shown in this c. 1940 scene from the Wiley Martin Sawmill near Deep Gap. Lumber from this area provided not only building materials for the Boone area, but for export as well. The virgin forests here were once covered in white pine, oaks, popular, ash, birch, beech, maple, hickory, and even chestnut. (Courtesy Claude Bodenhamer, original by Paul Weston with Boone Photo Shop.)

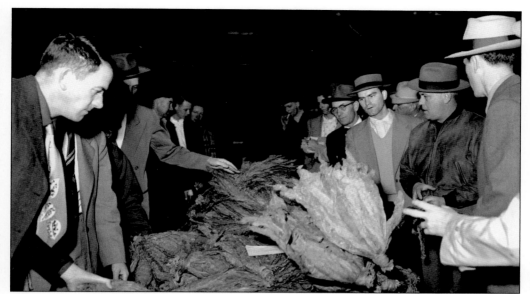

BUYERS INSPECTING TOBACCO AT MARKET. In this photograph, buyers examine the tobacco crop at market. Burley tobacco was first planted here in 1929, but the plant adjusted well to the climate and soils. By 1929, Watauga County had its first tobacco warehouse. In the 1970s, tobacco was king here and Watauga County was ranked sixth among 24 mountain counties in tobacco production. However, as allotments have decreased and finding labor is more difficult, fewer farmers are growing tobacco. Many farmers are searching for a replacement cash crop and experimenting with organic produce and other products. (Courtesy George Flowers and Boone Chamber of Commerce.)

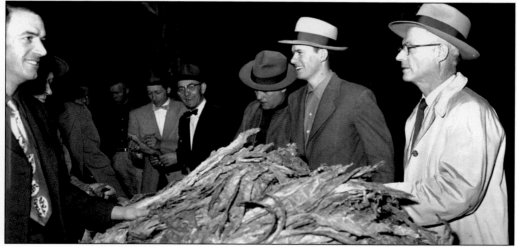

TOBACCO MARKET IN THE 1950S. Burley tobacco quickly caught on as a cash crop in the mountains after 1929. Several tobacco warehouses were located in the downtown area at one time. Watauga County continues to rank high among mountain counties in tobacco production. At market, the farmers waited anxiously to hear the prices they would receive for their crop. This tobacco money often paid the mortgage and farm payment. Today, the tobacco market is being replaced by direct contracts between farmers and tobacco companies. (Courtesy George Flowers and Boone Chamber of Commerce.)

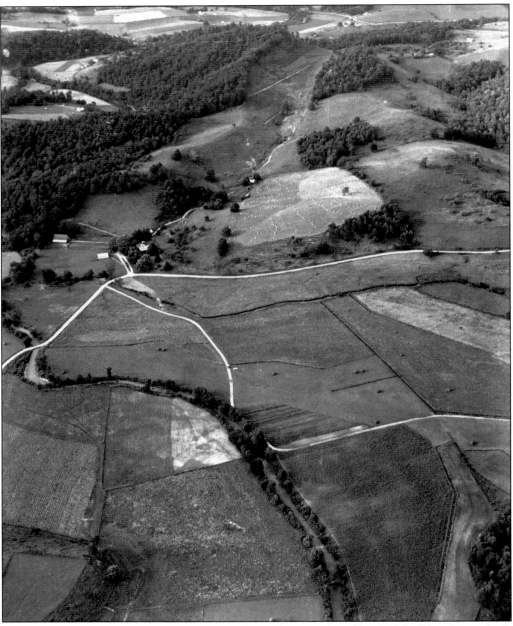

BLAIR HOME AND AERIAL VIEW. This view shows the agricultural land of the Blair Farm which was developed into the Boone Golf Course. As land values have escalated in the mountains, more farmers have sold land for development. Crops grown on the Blair Farm included cabbage, potatoes, apples, corn, and grains. The Blair House (built in 1844) and barn are on the upper left of the photograph. The Blair House still sits off Deerfield Road, a reminder of a bygone age. (Courtesy Sarah Blair Spencer.)

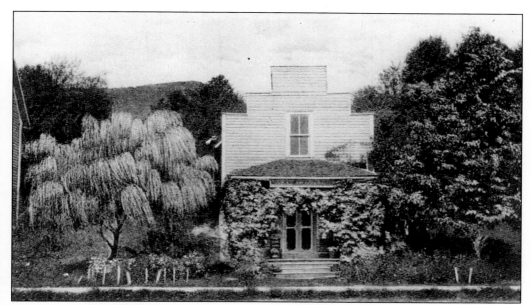

MISS JENNIE COFFEY'S STORE. This store was located along the north side of King Street near the present post office. Miss Jennie not only sold hats but also schoolbooks to area pupils in the early 1900s. (Courtesy Historic Boone.)

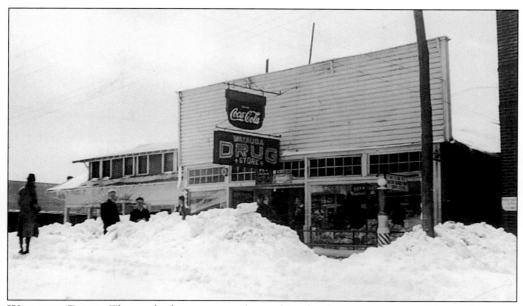

WATAUGA DRUG. This early drugstore was located in the downtown area and located next to the Greene Inn. Neither building has lasted through time. The barber pole on the right of the building indicates a barber's shop in the building. (Courtesy Historic Boone.)

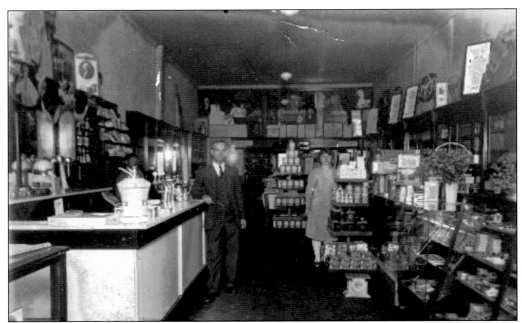

BOONE DRUG. This company was founded in 1919 by G.K. Moose in its first downtown location. It was incorporated in 1939, and Dr. Moose owned the company for about 50 years. The store has become a tradition in the area and is one of the oldest continuous businesses in downtown Boone. Boone Drugs today has seven stores in the area. (Courtesy Boone Drug.)

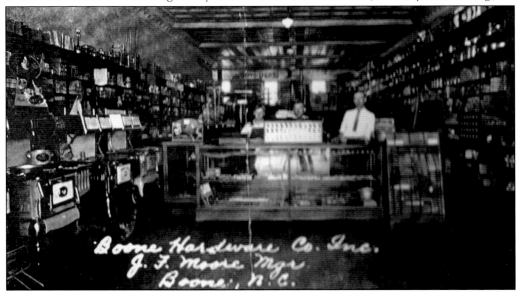

BOONE HARDWARE STORE INTERIOR. This photograph shows (from left to right) Ruth Cottrell, Troy Norris, and J. Frank Moore, the manager. Boone Hardware was owned by Russell Hodges and Clyde Greene and was the predecessor to Farmer's Hardware. This photo shows the original counter, still in Farmer's Hardware today. These stores served a stronger social function in the community in the past than shopping at a chain store provides today. (Courtesy Historic Boone.)

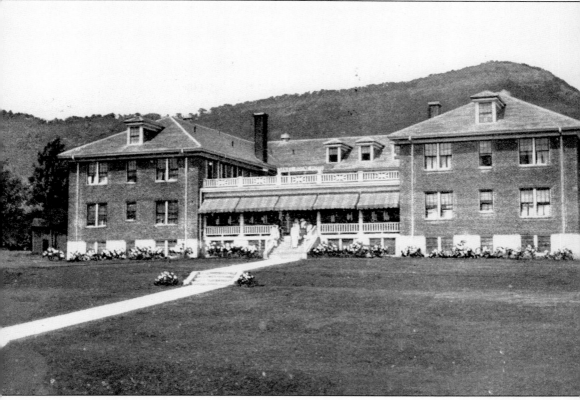

Daniel Boone Hotel. This postcard is postmarked 1931 and is addressed to Miss Violet McCrudden in Moorestown, New Jersey. It reads, "This is a very pretty place. I climbed a mountain this afternoon. See you soon. Mildred." The Daniel Boone Hotel was the ultimate in refinement for Boone, and hosted meetings, parties, and dances. The restaurant inside was a regular for Sunday dinners. Many locals and visitors enjoyed sitting on the porch and passing the time. The grand hotel was located on the north side of King Street in the current location of Daniel Boone Condominiums. The hotel was torn down in 1984, an action that is regretted by many today. The Daniel Boone Condominium development, named in honor of the old hotel, was constructed on the site in 1984. (Courtesy Richard Trexler.)

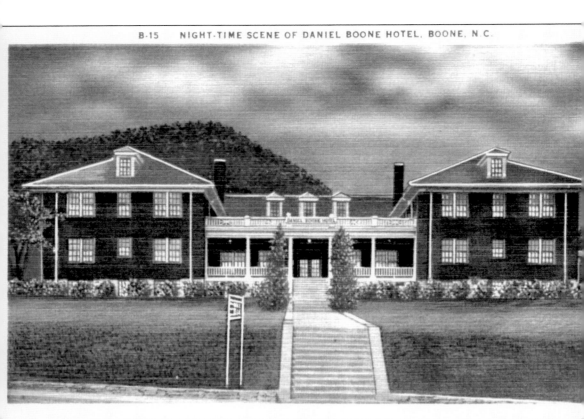

NIGHT-TIME SCENE OF DANIEL BOONE HOTEL. This postcard provides a romantic view of the hotel at night. Although Boone had only one of these grand hotels, neighboring Blowing Rock had several of them. The only remaining one of these grand dames in Blowing Rock is the Green Park Inn. This hotel was demolished in 1984, and had been allowed to deteriorate prior to that time. The grand Daniel Boone Hotel is remembered as a favorite gathering place and site for parties and dances. The Daniel Boone Condominium development was constructed in 1984 and provides multifamily housing for college students and town residents. (Courtesy Brian Lambeth.)

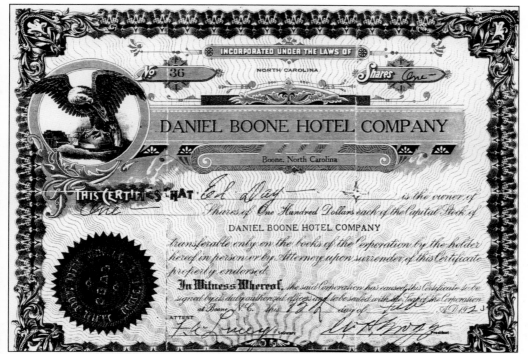

STOCK CERTIFICATE FOR DANIEL BOONE HOTEL COMPANY 1925. The share certificate of $100 for Ed Day bought one share of the Daniel Boone Hotel Company. This certificate represents the significance of the hotel to the town's economy. (Courtesy Historic Boone.)

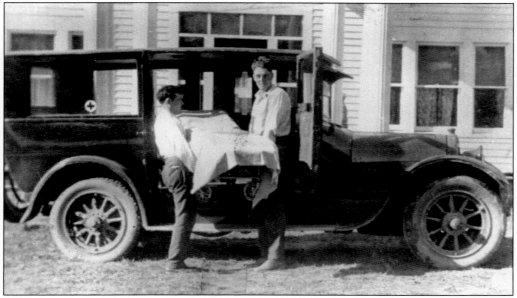

BOONE'S FIRST HOSPITAL, NOW DANIEL BOONE INN. This c. 1920 ambulance is pictured in front of the Bingham house, which later became the Daniel Boone Inn. The second hospital in Boone was located in Founders Hall on the Appalachian State University campus. (Courtesy Patt Paal and Daniel Boone Inn.)

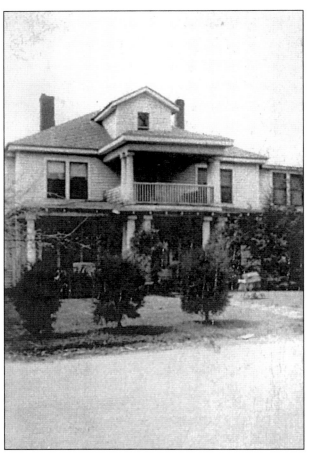

DR. BINGHAM HOME. This building was the home of Dr. Bingham, and was one of the first hospitals in Boone. The house was built in 1923 and once served as a private residence, hospital, and rooming house. It became a restaurant in 1959 and was operated by Mr. and Mrs. Whitaker from Wilkesboro. The front porch and back dining area were later additions. The main house was once used as sleeping quarters for employees. The present-day Daniel Boone Inn is famous for its family-style service and ham biscuits. (Courtesy Historic Boone.)

DANIEL BOONE RESTAURANT. Originally the residence of Dr. Bingham, this building has served as a hospital, rooming house, and, as it's most known for, a restaurant. Additions have been built on to the original building. This restaurant is a tradition for many tourists, college students, and locals who enjoy the large servings of country-style food. (Courtesy Appalachian Cultural Museum.)

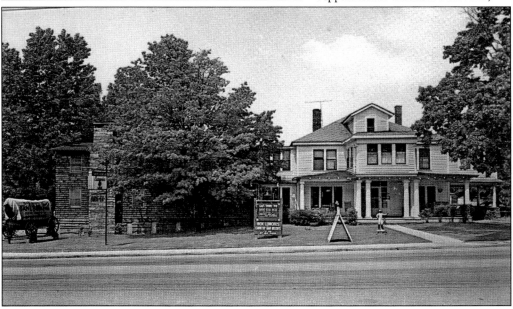

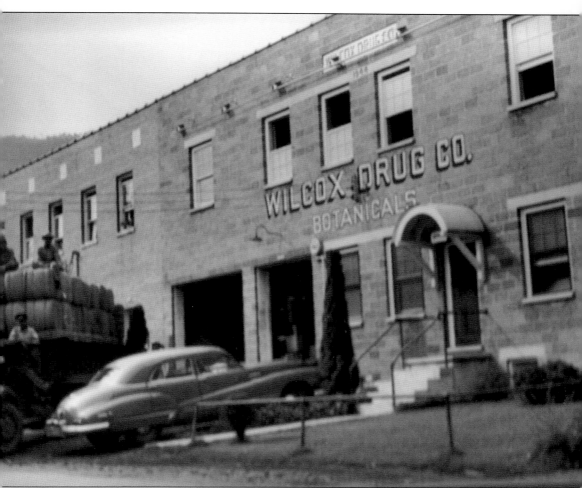

WILCOX DRUGS/NATURAL PRODUCTS. This photograph shows the Wilcox Drug Company building about 1950 in its location on Howard Street. The business was started by General Grant Wilcox in 1900 in Todd and moved to Boone in the 1940s. The business purchases botanicals and herbs from local gatherers and helped supplement incomes of farmers. The company, now North American Natural Products, deals with a limited number of natural items (mostly exported to Europe for herbal products) and evergreen treens and greenery. Their new office is located on Highway 194. This building has since become the Wilcox Emporium and restaurants. (Courtesy Chris Wilcox.)

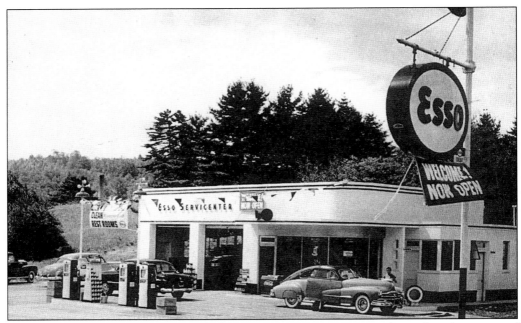

ESSO SERVICENTER IN 1950. The Shirley-Ragan Esso gas station was located at the corner of Hardin and Howard Streets, beside the Daniel Boone Restaurant. The garage is still operating but under a different fuel company. (Courtesy Historic Boone.)

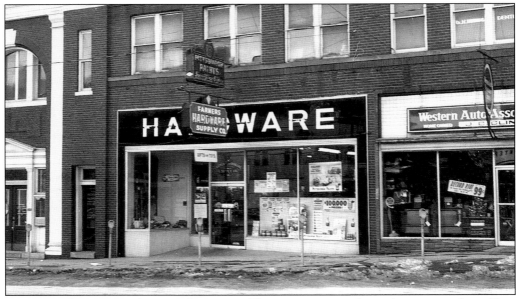

FARMERS HARDWARE SUPPLY COMPANY. This street scene shows businesses along King Street, including (from left to right) Northwestern Bank, Farmers Hardware, and Western Auto Associates. Dr. Farthings's dentist office was located upstairs from Western Auto. Now, Farmers' Hardware has expanded into the former bank building on the corner of Depot and King Streets. The hardware store is one of the few long-term businesses in downtown Boone. (Courtesy Historic Boone.)

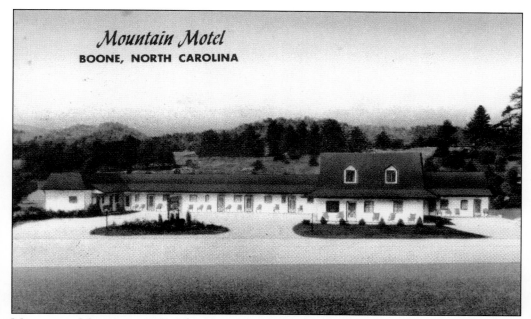

MOUNTAIN MOTEL IN 1953. The Mountain Motel, built by Mr. Tatum, was one of the first commercial motels in Boone to house the increasing number of tourists. It was located at the current location of McDonald's on U.S. 321. The mystique of the mountains is promoted in this postcard. It reads, "Mountain Motel Near Good Restaurant on U.S. Highways 221–321 New-Quiet-Restful-Private Baths." (Courtesy Appalachian Cultural Museum.)

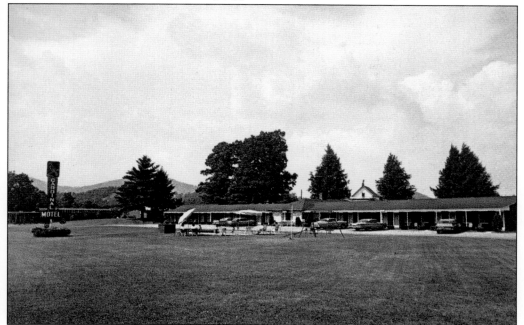

CARDINAL MOTEL. This postcard boasts, "ultra-modern accommodations in magnificent mountain setting." Mr. and Mrs. Gwyn Hayes are listed as the owners. This hotel is still located off Highway 421. (Courtesy Appalachian Cultural Museum.)

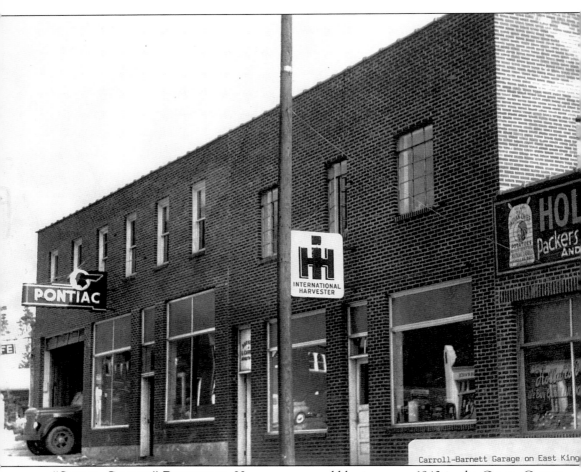

Carroll-Barnett Garage on East King

"GREASY CORNER" BUSINESSES. Here were some old businesses *c.* 1940 in the Greasy Corner area of Boone, at the intersection of Hardin and King Streets. The area was referred to as Greasy Corner because of several garages in the vicinity. Shown here are the Carroll-Barnett Garage and Hollar's Produce. These building still stand near the corner. (Courtesy Historic Boone.)

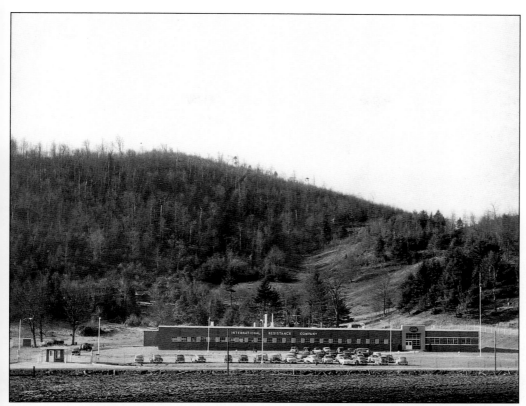

INTERNATIONAL RESISTANCE COMPANY (IRC) C. 1950. The first major manufacturing endeavor in Watauga County was the International Resistance Company, founded in 1953. The company opened with 44 employees and has long been a major employer in the area. The plant makes electronic parts for computers, automobiles, and wire data transmission lines. IRC is the largest employer in Boone, with the exception of the town and the university. (Courtesy Historic Boone.)

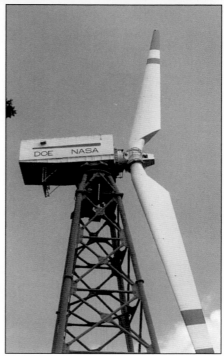

HOWARD'S KNOB WINDMILL. This giant windmill was erected on top of Howard's Knob in 1979 by NASA to generate electricity for Blue Ridge Electric Membership Corporation, the local utility company. The cost of construction and installation of the wind turbine was $29 million and it had 100-foot blades. One of the largest windmills in the world at that time, it was capable of producing up to 2,000 kilowatts and supplying energy to 500 homes in Boone area. Due to mechanical problems and funding cuts for wind-energy research, the windmill was dismantled in 1983. Many of the residents disliked the windmill and were happy to see it leave. (Courtesy Historic Boone.)

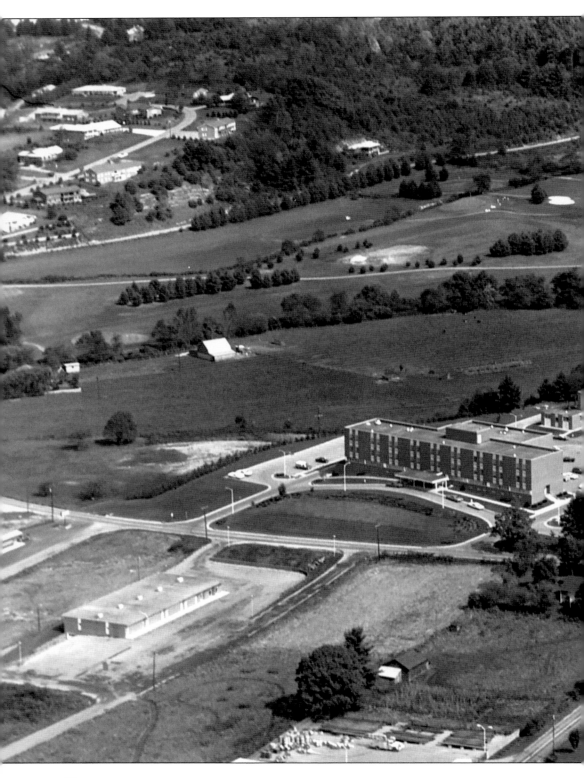

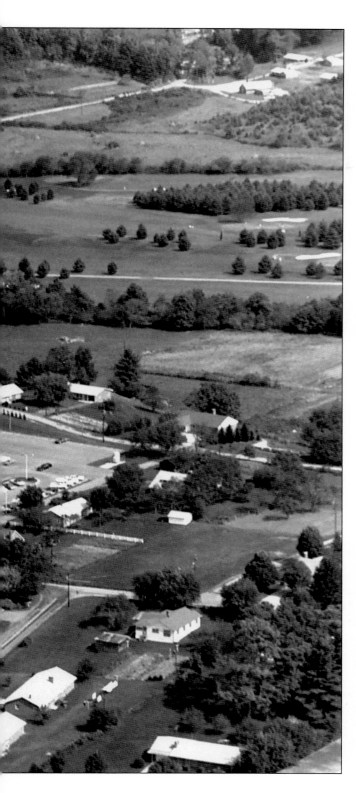

WATAUGA HOSPITAL. This aerial view of the Watauga Medical Center shows the low-density development which at first surrounded it. Today, this area still has some single-family housing, but many medical offices have been built nearby. The Medical Center was built in the mid-1960s. Additions were built in the mid-1970s, the early 1990s, and another one is underway in 2003. (Courtesy Watauga County Public Library; photographed by Henry DeWolf.)

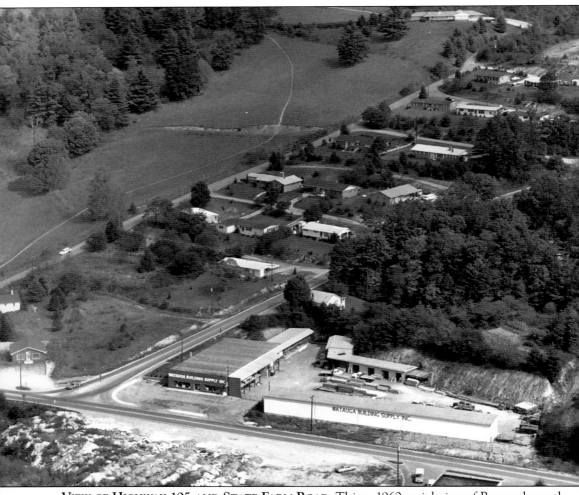

VIEW OF HIGHWAY 105 AND STATE FARM ROAD. This *c.* 1960 aerial view of Boone shows the changes which have taken place in the newer commercial and office areas of Boone. The road across the bottom of the photograph is the Highway 105 Extension and State Farm Road leads up from this road. The Watauga Building Supply business is still located at the intersection, but many new businesses have located along these major roads. Highway 105 was widened to four lanes as well. The residential area is still located in town. State Farm Road is developing as a medical office area, because of the proximity to the hospital. (Courtesy Watauga County Public Library; photographed by Henry DeWolf.)

Six

SCHOOLS AND ASU

Both schools and churches were necessities for settlers. One of the earliest schools was located by Boone Creek, near today's Appalachian State University. The Boone Academy was a successful early school in the area, established by 1868. In 1899, schools and academies in Watauga County included New River Academy, Cove Creek Academy, Skyland Institute at Blowing Rock, and Watauga Academy.

The history of Appalachian State University (ASU) is more closely linked to Boone's history than is the case with most college towns. Two local brothers, Dauphin Disco (D.D.) Dougherty and Blanford Barnard (B.B.) Dougherty, founded Watauga Academy in 1899, the predecessor to Appalachian State University. Watauga Academy began with 53 grammar school students and was located across from the current location of the ASU power plant. The school first provided only a grammar education, but later added high school classes.

With an eagerness and determination to provide quality education, the townspeople donated funds and supplies for the early school. After 1903, it became Appalachian Training School and received state funding. In 1921, the name was changed to Appalachian State Normal School, and again in 1929 it was changed to Appalachian State Teachers College. The small college offered a wide variety of educational, cultural, and athletic activities. Able and talented college presidents and chancellors provided excellent leadership and vision. In 1967, the school became Appalachian State University. The college has continued to grow, adding students, more programs of studies, and university facilities. With an enrollment of 14,050 students, the school still seems like a community, surrounded by the sheltering mountains. It is ranked as one of the best public colleges in the South, an accomplishment of which the Dougherty brothers would have been proud.

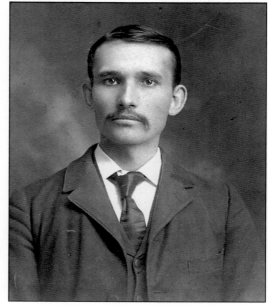

B.B. DOUGHERTY. Along with his brother D.D, B.B. Dougherty founded Watauga Academy in 1899, which has evolved into Appalachian State University. These two brothers had a vision for an exemplary school in the mountains. (Courtesy Historic Boone.)

85

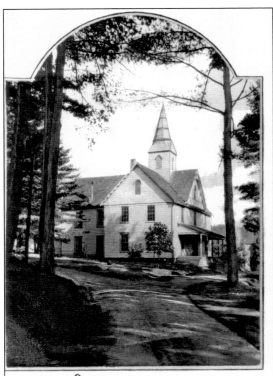

WATAUGA ACADEMY, A.T.S.

WATAUGA ACADEMY, A.T.S. This is the building where Appalachian State University has its roots. Daniel Baker Dougherty (father of B.B. and D.D.) and J.F. Hardin donated the land and the local townspeople donated over $1,000 for this building. The Academy, located across from the current location of the ASU power plant, opened with 53 grammar school students. High school classes were added later. (Courtesy University Archives and Records, Appalachian State University.)

FACULTY AT APPALACHIAN TRAINING SCHOOL. Dauphin Disco (D.D.) Dougherty is shown on the left of the photograph and Blanford Barnard (B.B.) Dougherty is on the far right. These two men established Watauga Academy in 1899. The other faculty are not identified. In its early history, the rules and policies for the academy and training school were strict, and these men look capable of enforcing them. (Courtesy University Archives and Records, Appalachian State University.)

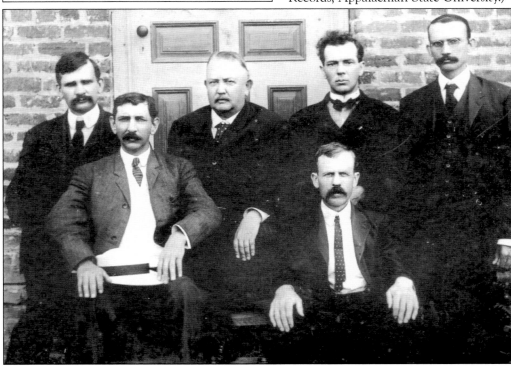

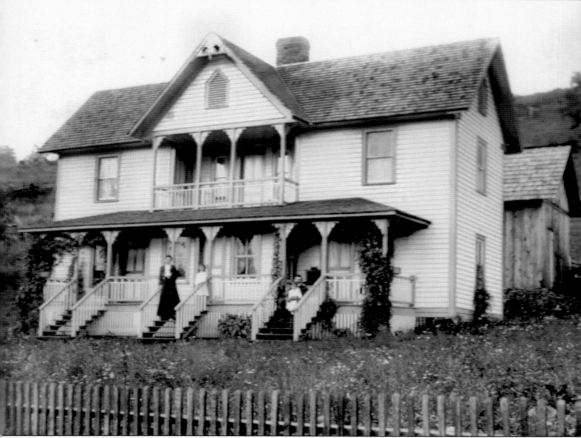

THE DOUGHERTY HOUSE C. 1905. The home of the Dougherty family, who started Appalachian State University, was built about 1903. It was located along present-day Rivers Street near Stadium Drive. The house was ornately decorated for that time period. An outbuilding, probably a springhouse, is partially visible behind the house. The house was later remodeled, enlarged, and moved to a site off U.S. Highway 321 near Tweetsie Railroad. The building now houses the Appalachian Heritage Museum. In spite of the push for new development, the university acted responsibly by preserving the historic home. (Courtesy University Archives and Records, Appalachian State University.)

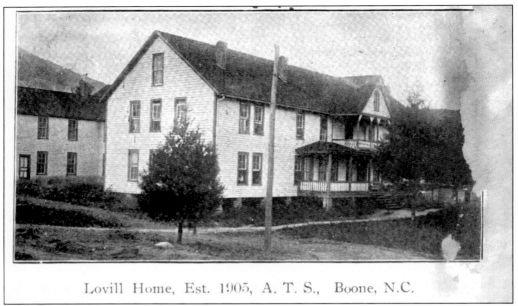

Lovill Home, Est. 1905, A. T. S., Boone, N.C.

LOVILL HOME, EST. 1905, A.T.S. This early postcard pictures the Lovill Home at Appalachian Training School, which stood northeast of Founders Hall. The postcard was addressed to Miss Bess Wilson in Knoxville, Tennessee. This building, constructed in 1915, was used for a women's dormitory. It no longer exists. (Courtesy Anna Boyce Phillips.)

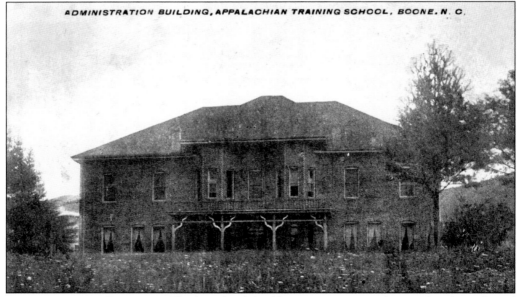

ADMINISTRATION BUILDING, APPALACHIAN TRAINING SCHOOL, BOONE. N. C.

ADMINISTRATION BUILDING. The large brick building was constructed in 1905 and stood until 1924 near the current location of Founders Hall. Postmarked 1912, this postcard shows the first Administration Building at the Training School. Addressed to Miss Bessie Wilson in Zionville, North Carolina, it reads, "Say, don't you think I have never got that shirt fixed yet. Mama says she is not going to fix it for I ought to have known better than to have been playing with girls. I will know better next time. Ha! Best wishes, J.C.F." (Courtesy Anna Boyce Phillips.)

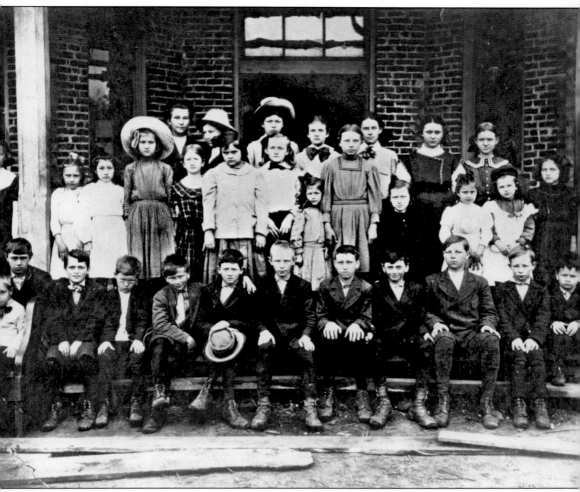

CLARA BARTLETT DOUGHERTY'S C. 1910 A.T.S. CLASS. Ms. Dougherty is seen on the top row, second from right. This elementary class appears to be posed in front of the first Administration Building. (Courtesy University Archives and Records, Appalachian State University.)

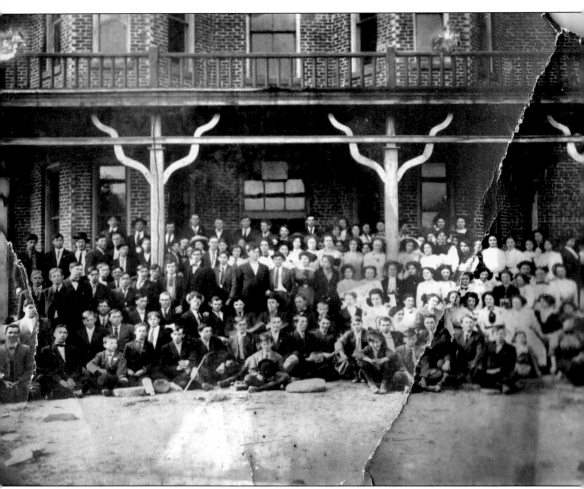

CLASS AT APPALACHIAN TRAINING SCHOOL, C. 1911. This class is posed in front of the old Administration Building. This grand brick building had a hipped roof and unusual curved porch supports. The first administration building was located to the north of present-day Founders Hall in the curve of the campus road. (Courtesy Historic Boone.)

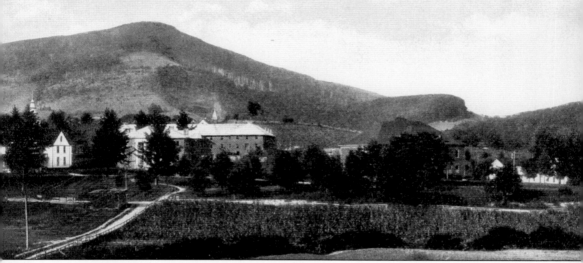

ppalachian Training School, Boone, N. C.

Watauga Bldg.   Science Hall   New Dormitory   Administration Bldg.   Lovill House

APPALACHIAN TRAINING SCHOOL, C. 1920. This postcard shows (from left to right) the Watauga Building (Academy), Science Hall, New Dormitory, Administration Building, and Lovill House. For many years, this row of buildings was the main campus. All of the buildings are gone now. (Courtesy Richard Trexler.)

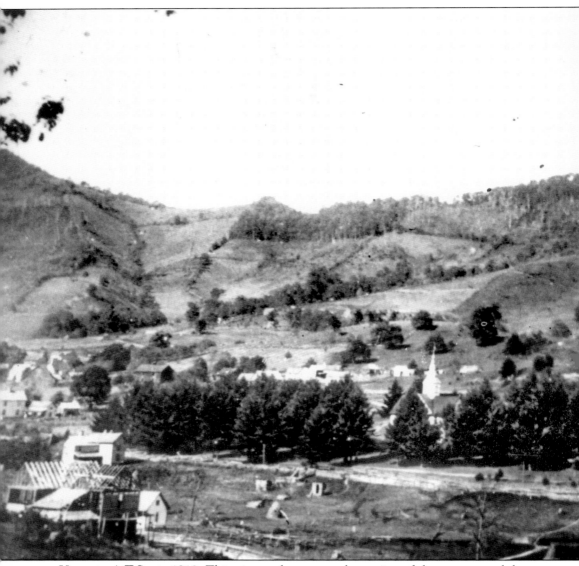

VIEW OF **A.T.S.,** c. **1910.** This picture shows a northern view of the campus and downtown. The first Administration Building can be seen in the right of the photograph. On the left, the building with the steeple is Watauga Academy. Next to the Administration building is the

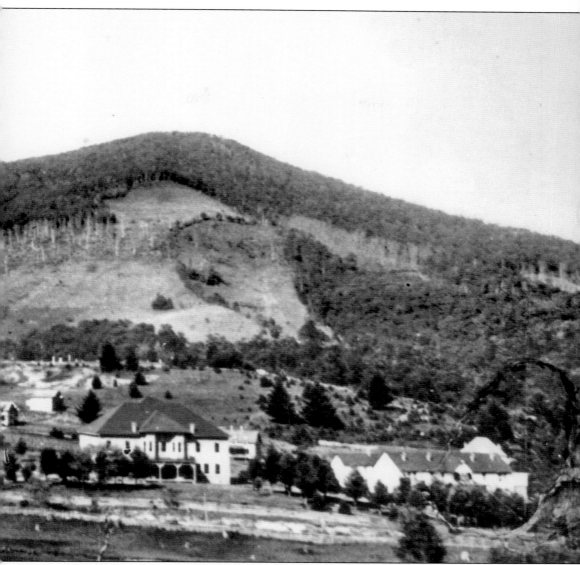

Lovill house. Howard's Knob is in the background. (Courtesy University Archives and Records, Appalachian State University.)

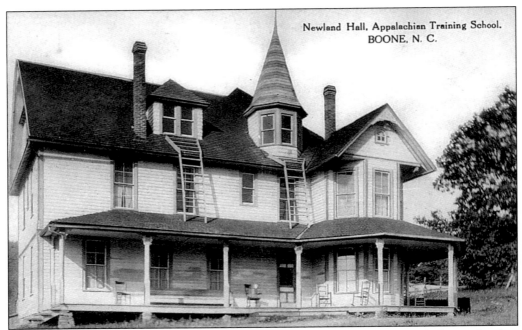

Newland Hall, Appalachian Training School.
BOONE, N. C.

NEWLAND HALL, APPALACHIAN TRAINING SCHOOL. This early postcard shows the first Newland Hall, built in 1908. It was the first men's dormitory. The second Newland Hall was built in 1939. (Courtesy Historic Boone.)

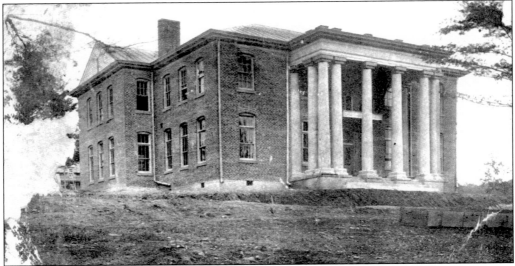

NEW SCIENCE HALL, APPALACHIAN TRAINING SCHOOL, BOONE, NORTH CAROLINA. This postcard shows the old science hall which stood from 1911 until 1946. The building was located between the first administration building and Watauga Academy, north of present-day Founders Hall. The card is addressed to Miss Bess Wilson in Knoxville, Tennessee. It reads, "My dear little girl, How are you? I long so much to have just a word from you. I do hope you will soon be well, and back with us. [Illegible word] if I could just run in on you some day and have a good old racket like we used to have at home. Bess, you had better have someone to write me. Don [illegible last name]." (Courtesy Anna Boyce Phillips.)

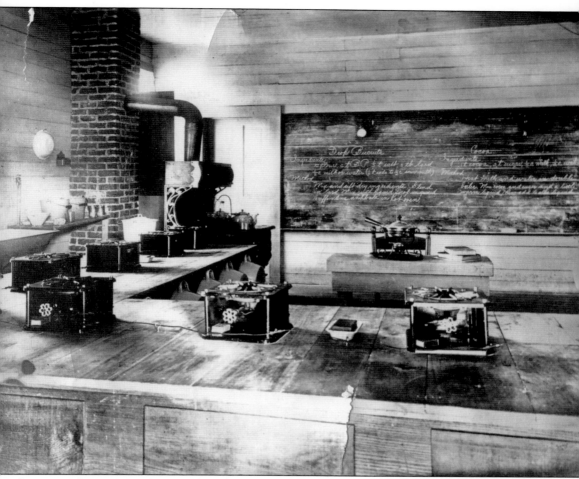

COOKING CLASSROOM A.T.S. This photograph shows the classroom for a cooking class at Appalachian Training School in about 1915. The recipe for drop biscuits and cocoa is written on the chalkboard. Classes in many domestic skills were offered at the school in the early days. Note the old stove with ornate ironwork in the corner. (Courtesy University Archives and Records, Appalachian State University.)

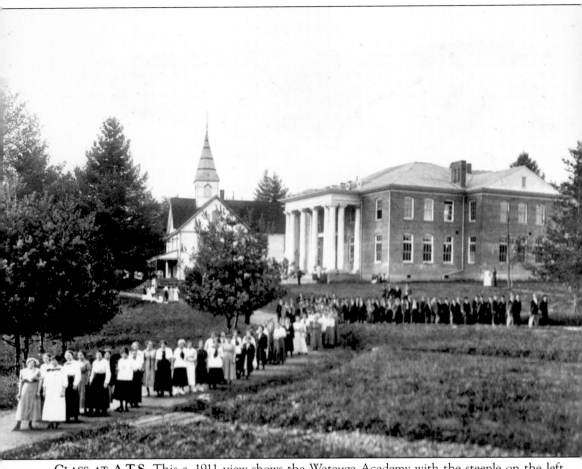

CLASS AT A.T.S. This *c.* 1911 view shows the Watauga Academy with the steeple on the left and the old Science Building, built in 1911. This is a nice view of the original campus with students lined up. (Courtesy University Archives and Records, Appalachian State University.)

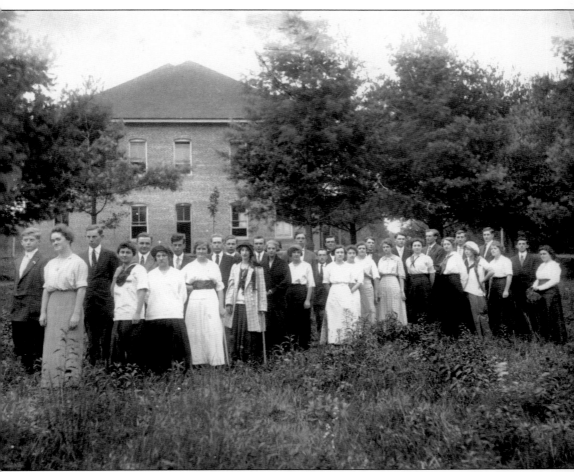

CLASS OF 1916. This image was taken at south end of the first administration building. The class is ready for an outing, perhaps to Howard's Knob in spring of 1916. The first couple is (from left to right) Fitzhugh Hurley and Thelma Truitt; (second couple) Grant Donnelly and Hatt Choate; (third group) Cloy Winkler and Dare Phillips (Mrs. Strother), Alverta Phillips; (fourth couple) Dean Bingham and Carrie Horton (Mrs. Dean Bingham); (fifth couple) Tracy Councill and Dora Greer; (sixth group) Russell D. Hodges and Faye Greer (Mrs. Russell D. Hodges), unidentified and Elma McGuire; (eighth couple) unidentified and Mattie Seitz; (ninth couple) Robert Dickson and Mary Payne; (tenth couple) unidentified and Carrie Coffey; (eleventh couple) T. Edgar Sikes and Rebecca Osborne; (twelfth couple) George R. Sherrill and Lula Wilson (Mrs. Houck Richards); (thirteenth couple) unidentified and Bertha Greene; (fourteenth couple) Walter Sullivan and Zora Woodie; and (fifteenth couple) Roderick Love and Ila Osborne. (Courtesy University Archives and Records, Appalachian State University.)

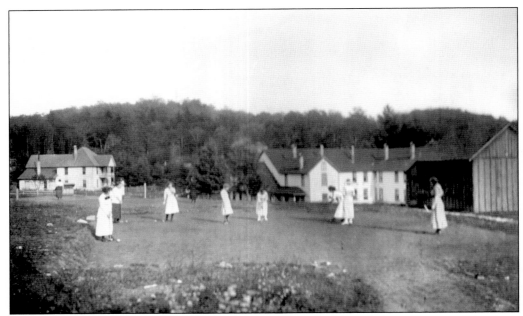

WOMEN PLAYING CROQUET C. 1920. These young ladies of Appalachian Training School are playing a leisurely game of croquet in front of Lovill Home Dorm, on the right of the image. On the left is the Bynum McNeil house, which was later destroyed by fire. (Courtesy University Archives and Records, Appalachian State University.)

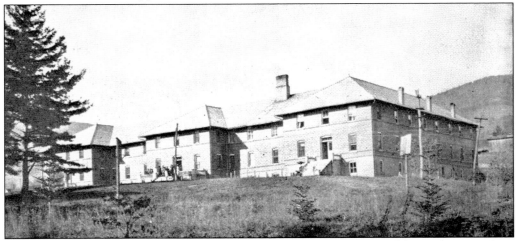

WHITE HALL, A.T.S. White Hall Dormitory was built in 1924 and located across from the current location of Wellborn Cafeteria. This postcard is postmarked July 1922 and is addressed to Miss Winona Hethcox (?) in Matthews, North Carolina. "Dear Miss Winona, Please don't think I have forgotten you. I have never had to work anything like as hard at a summer school as I am doing here. Billie and me they put it on us good and heavy. Wish you were with us to enjoy the climate. It is cooler than Asheville. I think I am almost shivering now and the wind roars like it might be snowing. Am going to write you a letter soon, maybe tomorrow. May S." Appalachian started offering summer schools to attract students to the area, but perhaps the workload and weather were a bit too challenging for this correspondent. (Courtesy Richard Trexler.)

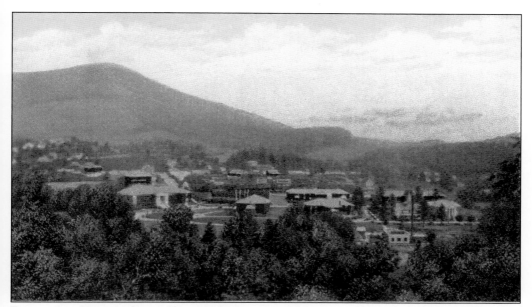

PANORAMIC VIEW OF STATE TEACHER'S COLLEGE. This postcard provides a view of the campus around 1940. The second administration building is the tall brick building on the left with white columns. To the right is the Dauph Blan dormitory and then White Hall. The card was published by the Asheville Post Card Co. (Courtesy Brian Lambeth.)

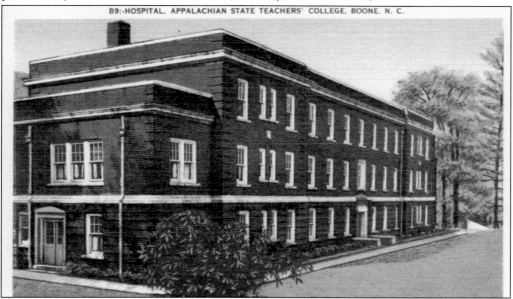

HOSPITAL, APPALACHIAN STATE TEACHERS' COLLEGE. Founders Hall was built in 1932 as a WPA project. Although Dr. Bingham's house was a hospital previous to construction of this building, Founders Hall was the county's first official hospital and also served as the college infirmary. This building provided a strong link between the community and the college. Fortunately, the university has preserved the building and it houses the personnel office today. (Courtesy Brian Lambeth and University Archives and Records, Appalachian State University.)

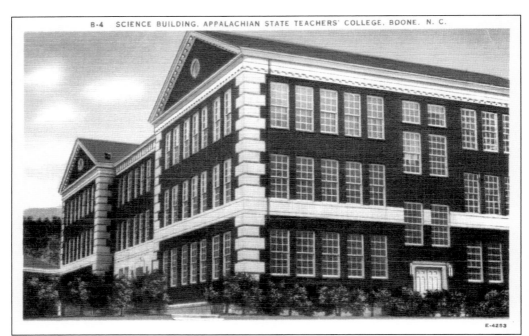

SCIENCE BUILDING, APPALACHIAN STATE TEACHERS' COLLEGE. This postcard shows the science building constructed in 1940 and located to the north of D.D. Dougherty building. The building was later named Smith-Wright. (Courtesy Brian Lambeth.)

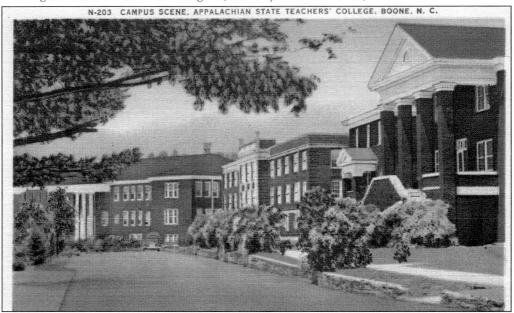

CAMPUS SCENE, APPALACHIAN STATE TEACHERS' COLLEGE. This postcard was made about 1940 and shows the beautiful brick buildings on the campus. From left to right, the buildings are the second Administration building (1924–1966), Dauph Blan dormitory (1929–?), and White Hall (1924–?). White Hall was originally a girls' dormitory. None of the buildings in this postcard remain. (Courtesy Brian Lambeth.)

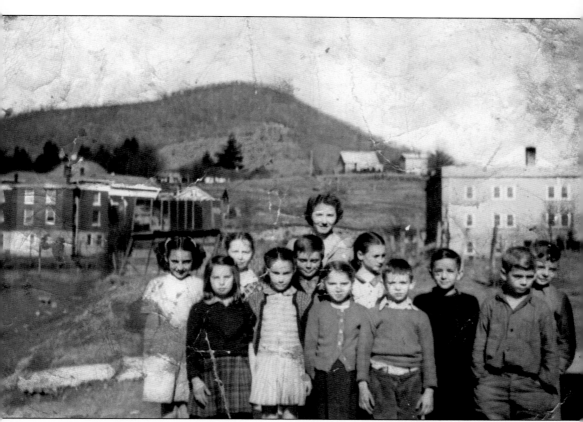

BOONE ELEMENTARY SCHOOL, 1942. Located on the campus of Appalachian State Teachers College, the elementary school provided education for local students and a learning environment for teachers in training. Student teachers from the college often assisted in the classrooms. This photograph is of one of the two fourth-grade classes at Boone Elementary. John T. Howell was the principal at this time. Pictured from left to right are (front row) Peggy Honeycutt (Mains), Romona Hardy (Jones), Lenore Greene (Critcher), Kermit Dacus, and Clay Beshears; (second row) Winona Buchanan, Betty Ray Greene (Koontz), Ernest Bolick, Sarah Jane Lewis, Dixon Qualls, and Charles Keller. The teacher is Miss Ella Austin Beshears. The Boone United Methodist Church building can be seen on the left and the First Baptist Church is on the right. (Courtesy Peggy Honeycutt Mains.)

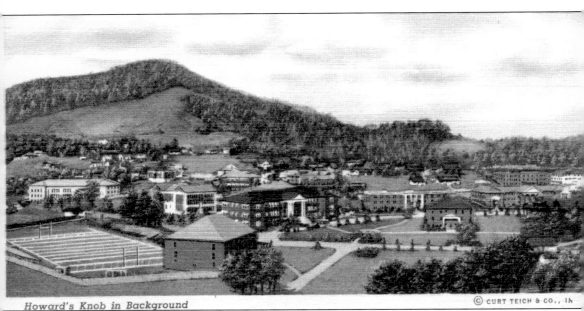

BIRD'S EYE VIEW OF APPALACHIAN STATE TEACHER'S COLLEGE, C. 1940. This view of the campus shows the Administration Building in the center. The football field is just to the left of that building. Above the football field is Chapel-Wilson (built in 1938) of Appalachian High School. The Science Hall (Smith Wright) appears to be behind the Administration Building. To the right of the Administration building are White Hall and East Hall. (Courtesy Richard Trexler.)

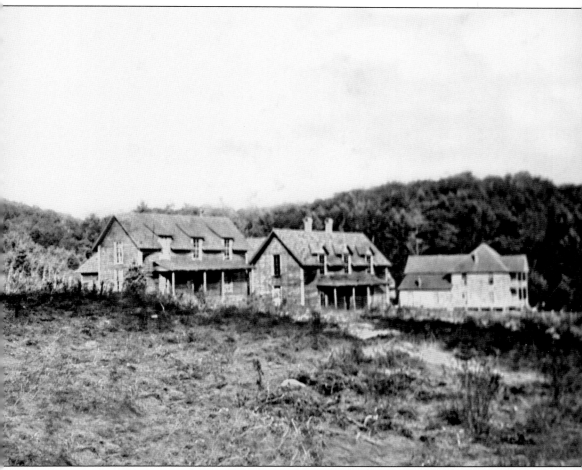

A.T.S. BOARDING HOUSES. Although the building on the left is unidentified, the next building is the McNeill House. Lovill Home Dorm is on the far right of the photograph. These dormitory buildings were across from the present location of Wellborn Cafeteria. (Courtesy University Archives and Records, Appalachian State University.)

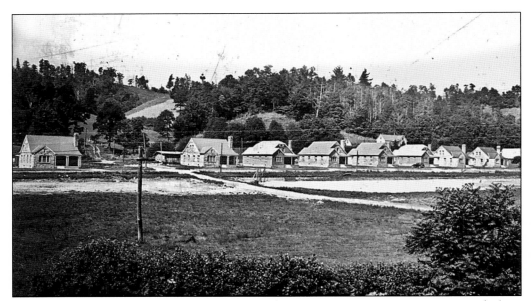

FACULTY HOUSING ALONG RIVERS STREET. These quaint cottages were constructed along Rivers Street in the 1940s and served as faculty housing and then college offices for many years. The buildings were demolished in the late 1990s to make way for new college buildings. (Courtesy Historic Boone.)

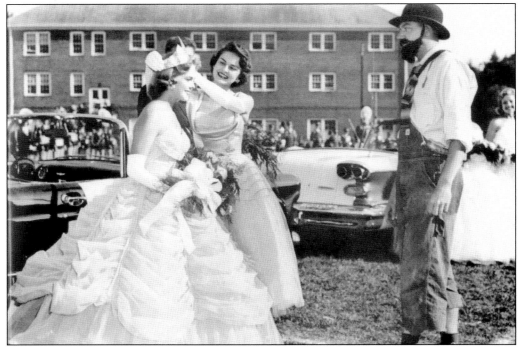

HOMECOMING QUEEN ESCORTED BY YOSEPH, C. 1955. In this photograph, a beautiful lady at Appalachian is crowned as queen while her escort, the mascot Yosef, awaits her. Carolyn Taylor, the reigning queen, is crowning the unidentified homecoming queen. (Courtesy University Archives and Records, Appalachian State University.)

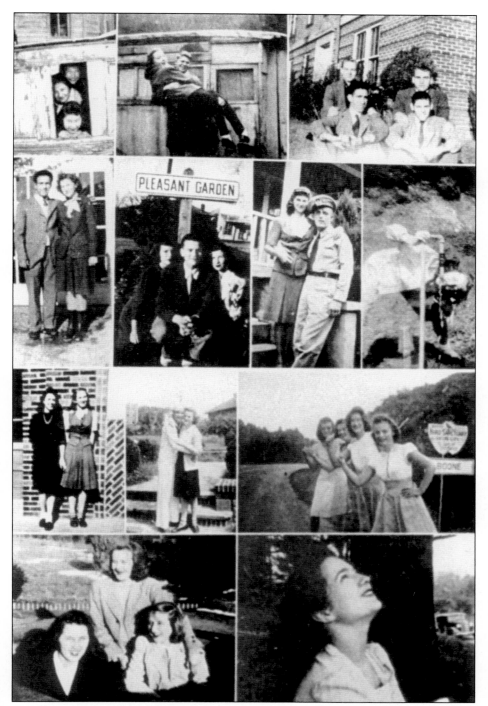

SCHOOL COLLAGE, C. 1945. These students seem to enjoy their campus life. Several soldiers are shown with sweethearts. The relaxed and friendly atmosphere on campus continues to be a major draw for students. (Courtesy University Archives and Records, Appalachian State University.)

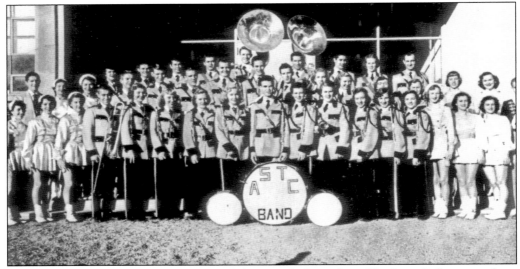

ASTC BAND, C. 1950. This image is of the Appalachian State Teachers College marching band. The school is still known for its excellent music program and marching band. (Courtesy University Archives and Records, Appalachian State University.)

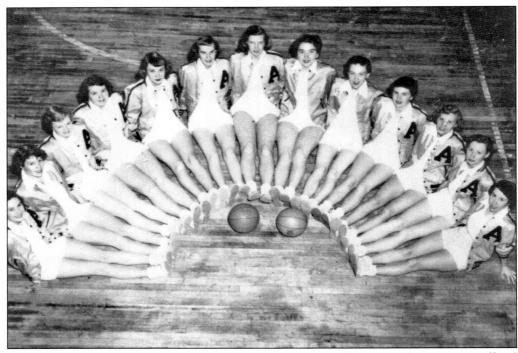

A.T.S. GIRLS' BASKETBALL TEAM, C. 1945. Sports teams and intramural sports were offered to students from the beginnings of the college. These activities continue to be popular today as well. (Courtesy University Archives and Records, Appalachian State University.)

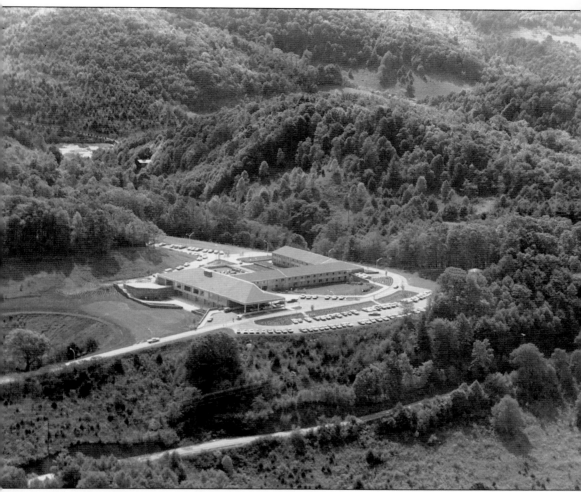

BROYHILL INN AND CONFERENCE CENTER. The Broyhill Center is part of Appalachian State University and offers pleasant accommodations and a state-of-art conference facility. The facility was constructed in 1972 as a residential center for continuing education. It is located on a hill overlooking the university. The university owns much of the forested land surrounding the center and allows it to be used for recreation. (Courtesy Watauga County Public Library.)

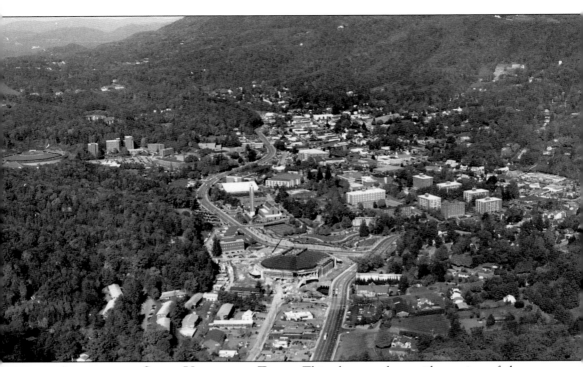

APPALACHIAN STATE UNIVERSITY TODAY. This photograph provides a view of the campus today. U.S. Highway 321 is shown running roughly straight up the photograph, and Rivers Street is the road on the left. The Convocation Center is the large building under construction in the foreground. The stadium can be seen on the left of the photograph near several multistory dormitories. (Courtesy Public Affairs, Appalachian State University.)

Seven

FRIENDS AND NEIGHBORS

Pioneers here must have been hardier than your average settler, as they dealt with steep terrain, isolation, and the harsh weather conditions of the area. Many of the settlers were of Scotch-Irish, Scottish, Irish, German, English, Welsh, and Swiss descent. Early families instrumental in settling and developing Boone included the Councils, the Coffeys, the Greenes, the Bryans, and the Blairs. Other families involved in the history of the town included the Cookes, Greers, Graggs, Doughertys, Hagamans, Winklers, Farthings, Critchers, Blackburns, Hodges, Linneys, and Rivers. Many of these names live on today among their descendants and geographic names in the area. Different kinds of people enabled Boone to become the successful, unique community of today, including farmers, business owners, tradesmen, teachers, and college students. It is only through their hard work that Boone has transformed itself from a "lost settlement" to one of the "best small towns in America."

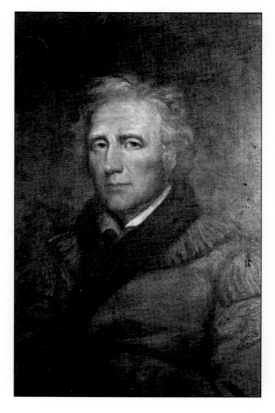

DANIEL BOONE. No book about Boone is complete without acknowledging its namesake. Although his connection has been promoted, Boone was likely only a transient visitor through the High Country. Born in Pennsylvania, Boone moved to Rowan County, North Carolina in 1750. He crossed this area of northwestern North Carolina in the 1760s on hunting expeditions and used the Howard cabin as a base for trips (the site is now on the ASU campus). He explored Kentucky for several years and helped open this new frontier for settlement. Boone went bankrupt in Kentucky and then moved to Spanish Missouri for new opportunities. (Courtesy Appalachian Cultural Museum.)

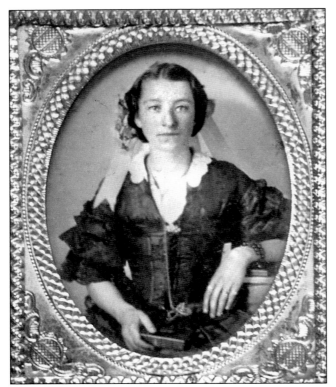

NANCY REBECCA BLAIR C. 1870. Beautiful Rebecca Blair was born c. 1835 and died about 1920. Rebecca married William Horton, who later served in the House of Commons in North Carolina. She lived in the Blair house, dating from 1844, which still stands along Deerfield Road across from the Boone Golf Course. The Blairs owned many acres in that area and hauled produce down the mountain by wagon to sell. (Courtesy Anna Boyce Phillips.)

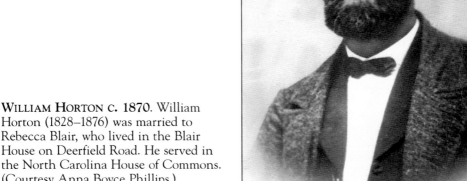

WILLIAM HORTON C. 1870. William Horton (1828–1876) was married to Rebecca Blair, who lived in the Blair House on Deerfield Road. He served in the North Carolina House of Commons. (Courtesy Anna Boyce Phillips.)

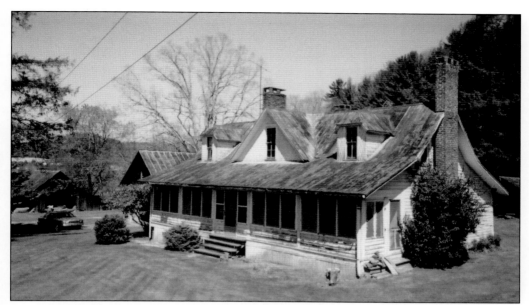

BLAIR HOME. This rustic farmhouse, dating from 1844, is one of the few reminders of Boone's agricultural past. Constructed of heart pine and hemlock, the house is located off Deerfield Road across from the Boone Golf Course. The house has remained in the Blair family. The farm raised cabbage, potatoes, apples, and fruit. Neal Blair can remember his father taking wagonloads of produce, dried beef, ham, and pork to Hickory, Morganton, Statesville, Charlotte, Gastonia, and Chester, South Carolina to sell. The Boone Golf Course and the Boone airport were developed on some of the extensive farmland of the Blair farm. (Courtesy Sarah Blair Spencer.)

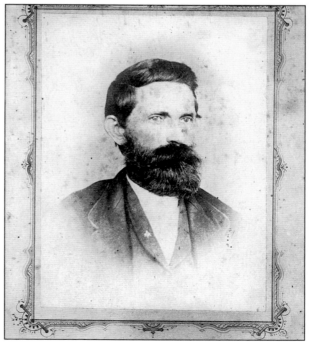

DR. JAMES GRAY RIVERS. Dr. Rivers, who arrived in Boone in 1865, was one of the town's earliest physicians. Born in Virginia, he was a Mason and son of Samuel and Rebecca Rivers. The doctor made house calls usually on horseback to traverse the rough mountain roads. Dr. Rivers' son, Robert Campbell, began the *Watauga Democrat* in 1889, along with Mr. Dougherty. The *Democrat* was published by Rivers until his death in 1933, when his son R.C. Rivers Jr. took over. After his death in 1975, his daughter Rachel Rivers-Coffey began operation of the paper with her husband Armfield Coffey. In the past few years, the newspaper was sold to a publishing company. (Courtesy Historic Boone.)

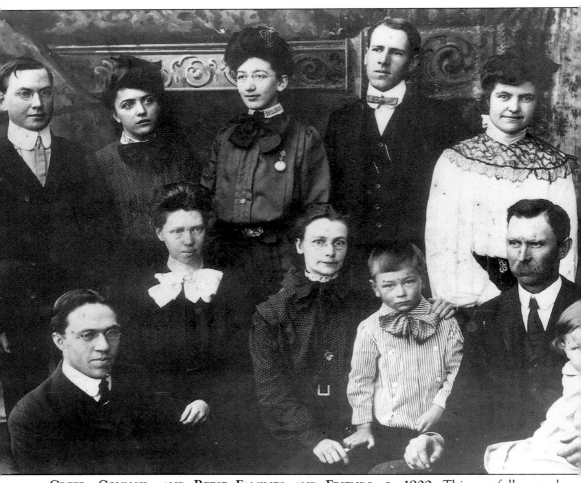

GREER, COUNCIL, AND REESE FAMILIES AND FRIENDS, C. 1900. This carefully posed photograph of townspeople includes several from old Boone families. I.G. Greer, the first person on the left in the front row, was an instructor at Appalachian Training School and a building on campus was named for him. Pictured from left to right are (front row) I.G. Greer, Bertha Eller, Mrs. B.J. Councill, Tracy Councill, B.J. Councill, and James Councill; (back row) Clyde Reese, unidentified, Miss Reese, G.P. Hagaman, and Margaret Sherrill. (Courtesy Historic Boone.)

ROMULUS ZACHARIAH LINNEY.
Romulus Zachariah Linney was a United
States Congressman and well-known
lawyer who spent summers in Boone.
He was also a Civil War veteran. Mr.
Linney was also a major supporter of
Appalachian Training School, now
Appalachian State University. His son,
Frank Armfield Linney, was United
States District Attorney and influential
in Boone politics. The Frank Armfield
Linney home still stands north of
King Street near the Water Street
intersection. (Courtesy Historic Boone.)

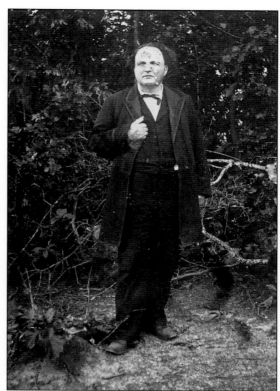

W.R. LOVILL. Mr. Lovill was an
attorney in Boone for many years.
Wade Brown, himself a longtime Boone
attorney, remembers Mr. Lovill always
wearing his trademark white fold-down
collar. His father was Capt. E.F. Lovill,
also an attorney. His office was located
on the south side of King Street near
the intersection with Water Street. Mr.
Lovill also served as mayor from 1939 to
1941. (Courtesy Historic Boone.)

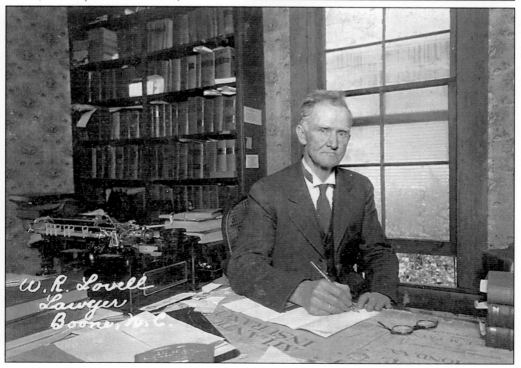

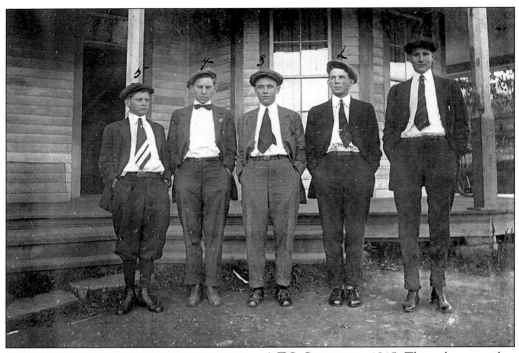

A.T.S. Students, 1915. These dapper male students are posed in front of old Justice Hall on the campus of Appalachian Training School in 1915. Pictured from left to right are Fitzhugh Hurley, Grant Donnelly, Russell Hodges, Frank Chappell, and Walter Sullivan. (Courtesy Historic Boone.)

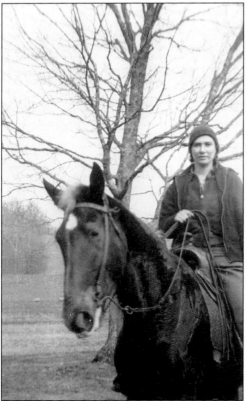

Addie Hardin Clawson, Mail Carrier. Addie Hardin Clawson delivered mail in Boone and Watauga County from 1936 until 1966 for a period of 30 years. In the early days, she had to ride a horse to deliver to rural routes and later on used an A-Model Ford on a route of 53 miles. Mrs. Clawson was dedicated to her customers and upon receiving a note from a mailbox, would often pick up and deliver medicine or groceries for those unable to get out. She was also known to deliver late Christmas gifts on Christmas Eve just so the children would receive their mailed presents. (Courtesy Rosalee Clawson Norris.)

GORDON H. WINKLER, MAYOR OF BOONE. Gordon Winkler is shown in this 1979 photograph. He was Boone's mayor from 1943 to 1961 and from 1969 to 1975 and oversaw much change in the town. The Winkler family has been very active in the community and contributed much to the area. (Courtesy Anna Boyce Phillips.)

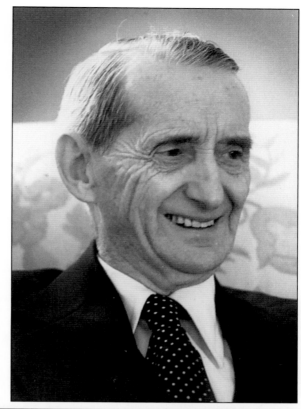

REV. RONDA HORTON. Rev. Horton (1895–1986) was a much-loved minister of the Boone Mennonite Brethren Church from about 1933 until 1984. He was a community leader of the Junaluska neighborhood. Reverend Horton was also an enterprising businessman and operated a coal yard and ice business just north of Queen Street. His love for people and generosity in helping those in need still lives on in memory. (Courtesy Historic Boone.)

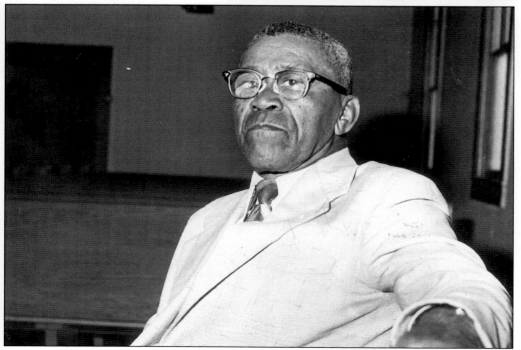

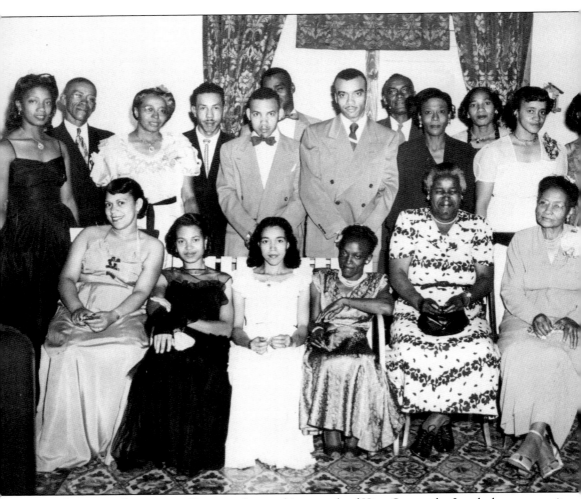

GROUP OF JUNALUSKA FRIENDS. Located just north of King Street, the Junaluska community is a tightly knit neighborhood of mainly African Americans. Most of the families have been there for several generations and it's one of the oldest intact historic neighborhoods in Boone. The Junaluska Heritage Foundation has been organized to preserve it history. From left to right are (front row) Katherine Folk, Marie Folk, Rachel Whittington, Martha Grimes, Della Horton, and Gertrude Folk; (middle row) Kerri Webb, Ruth Horton, Audie Folk, Lee Whittington, Lillie Whittington, Nell Ray, and Doretha Whittington; and (back row) Ronda Horton (minister of Boone Mennonite Brethren Church), Henry Clay Folk, John Henry Whittington, Martin Whittington, and Minnie White. (Courtesy Junaluska Heritage Foundation.)

Doc Watson, Traditional Musician. Award-winning performer Arthel "Doc" Watson still lives in Deep Gap, just outside the town of Boone. Although once a local picker, today Doc is known all over the world as an extraordinary roots musician. He is credited with the art of playing fiddle tunes on the flattop guitar. Doc has won five Grammy Awards, the National Medal of Arts, and a National Heritage Fellowship. He formed Merlefest, a popular roots music festival in Wilkesboro, to honor his deceased son, Merle Watson. The Doc Watson festival has been held in Cove Creek for the past six years. (Courtesy Folklore Productions.)

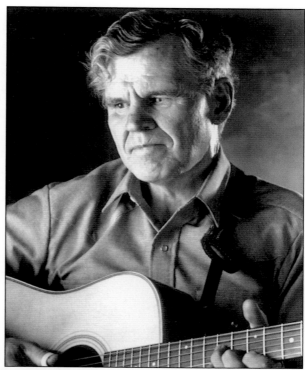

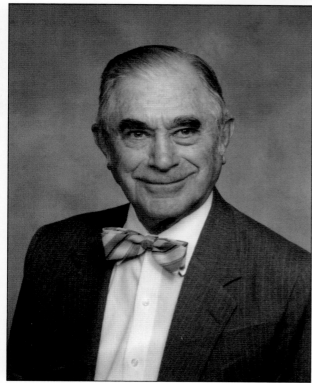

Wade E. Brown. Wade E. Brown, age 95, has been a longtime Watauga County resident and has seen the area grow from a peaceful town to a thriving tourist center and home of Appalachian State University. Wade Brown practiced law in downtown Boone for many years and was instrumental in the building of the Boone Golf Course. Mr. Brown has published his memoirs, titled *Recollections and Reflections*, a wonderful collection of stories of his life and experiences in the county. (Courtesy Wade Brown.)

Michael Cook
1849-1852

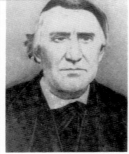
John (Jack) Horton
1852-1856
1866-1876

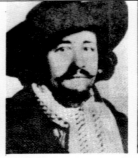
D.C. McCanless
1856-1860

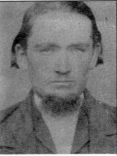
A.J. McBride
1860-1866
1876-1882

WATAUGA COUNTY SHERIFFS 1849–1882. These photographs show the succession of sheriffs of Watauga County. From left to right are Michael Cook (1849–1852) (no photo); John (Jack) Horton (1852–1856 and 1866–1876); D.C. McCanless (1856–1860); and A.J. McBride (1860–1866 and 1876–1882). (Courtesy Red Lyons and Watauga County Sheriffs Office.)

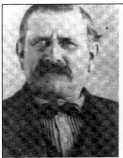
D.F. Baird
1882-1886
1890-1894

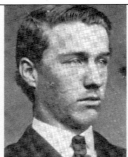
J.L. Hayes
1886-1890

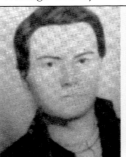
W.H. Calloway
1894-1900

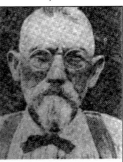
W.B. Baird
1900-1904

WATAUGA COUNTY SHERIFFS, 1882–1904. The following Watauga County sheriffs are shown from left to right: D.F. Baird (1882–1886) (1890–1894); J.L. Hayes (1886–1890); W.H. Calloway (1894–1900); and W.B. Baird (1900–1904). (Courtesy Red Lyons and Watauga County Sheriffs Office.)

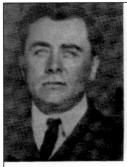
John W. Hodges Sr.
1904-1908

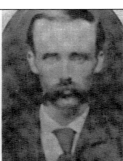
W.R. Ragan
1908-1912

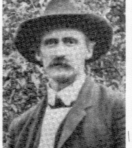
Asa Wilson
1912-1914

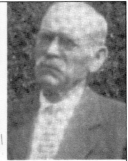
W.P. Moody
1914-1916

WATAUGA COUNTY SHERIFFS, 1904–1916. These photographs show the Watauga County sheriffs. From left to right are John W. Hodges Sr. (1904–1908); W.R. Ragan (1908–1912); Asa Wilson (1912–1914); and W.P. Moody (1914–1916). (Courtesy Red Lyons and Watauga County Sheriffs Office.)

118

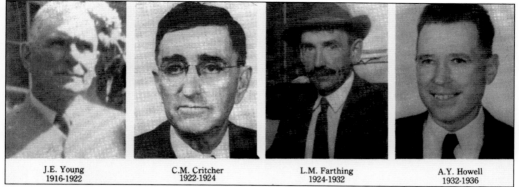

| J.E. Young | C.M. Critcher | L.M. Farthing | A.Y. Howell |
| 1916-1922 | 1922-1924 | 1924-1932 | 1932-1936 |

WATAUGA COUNTY SHERIFFS, 1916–1936. In this photograph are the following Watauga County sheriffs from left to right: J.E. Young (1916–1922); C.M. Critcher (1922–1944); L.M. Farthing (1924–1932); and A.Y. Howell (1932–1936). (Courtesy Red Lyons and Watauga County Sheriffs Office.)

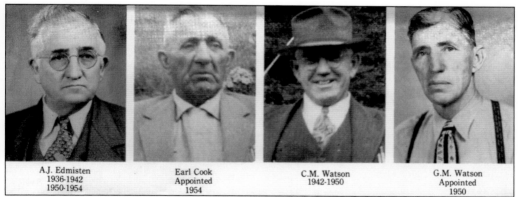

A.J. Edmisten	Earl Cook	C.M. Watson	G.M. Watson
1936-1942	Appointed	1942-1950	Appointed
1950-1954	1954		1950

WATAUGA COUNTY SHERIFFS 1936–1950. The following sheriffs of Watauga County are shown in this picture from left to right: A.J. Edmisten (1936–1942 and 1950–1954); Earl Cook (appointed 1954); C.M. Watson (1942–1950); and G.M. Watson (appointed 1950). (Courtesy Red Lyons and Watauga County Sheriffs Office.)

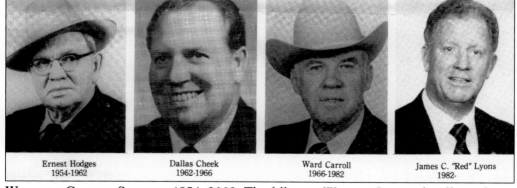

| Ernest Hodges | Dallas Cheek | Ward Carroll | James C. "Red" Lyons |
| 1954-1962 | 1962-1966 | 1966-1982 | 1982- |

WATAUGA COUNTY SHERIFFS 1954–2002. The following Watauga County sheriffs are shown from left to right: Ernest Hodges (1954–1962); Dallas Cheek (1962–1956); Ward Carroll (1966–1982); and James C. "Red" Lyons (1982–2002). (Courtesy Red Lyons and Watauga County Sheriffs Office.)

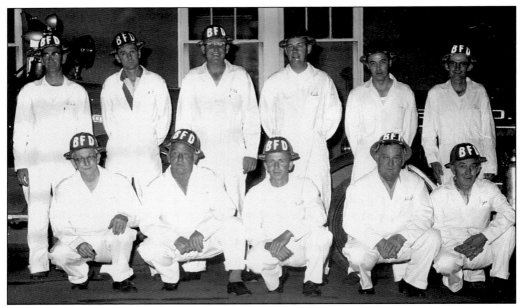

BOONE VOLUNTEER FIRE DEPARTMENT IN 1948. These dependable volunteers with the Boone Fire Department in 1948 are, from left to right, (front row) Lewis Reese, Howard Cottrell (Chief), Charles Blackburn, Raleigh Cottrell, and Joe Crawford; (back row) Grant Ayers, R.D. Hodges Jr., Phil Vance, Cecil Greene, Cecil Carter, and Cecil Farthing. The town organized a group to fight fires in 1926 and they have continued to provide brave, emergency service to the town. (Courtesy Boone Fire Department and Historic Boone.)

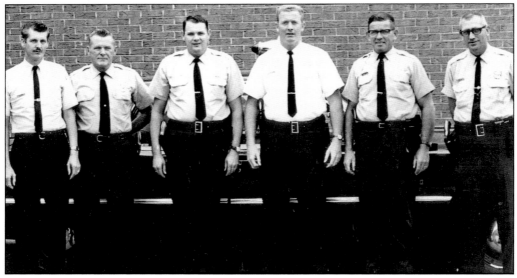

BOONE POLICE DEPARTMENT. The Boone Police Department has provided security for the town for many years. This 1968 photograph shows the force. From left to right are Jim Cannon, Stanley "Red" Burke, Hobert Watson, James "Red" Lyons, Mont Thomas, and Clarence "Frog" Greene. The 14,000 additional college students, summer visitors, and summer homeowners greatly add to the population of the town they are in charge of protecting. (Courtesy Boone Police Department.)

Eight

HIGH COUNTRY
ATTRACTIONS

The 1925 Directory of Boone sounds almost prophetic today, when it boasted, "a great many people are coming to this city to spend their summer vacations, where they can fish and hunt and have a good hotel, where they have good beds and plenty of palatable food at a very reasonable price." After transportation routes were in place, the High Country was discovered by tourists. Adjacent Blowing Rock boasted old stately hotels that attracted summer visitors even in the early 1900s. However, Boone's tourism industry grew more slowly and was tied to the growth of the university and the second-home market.

Tourists flocked to Boone to see the beautiful scenery from about the 1960s, but the tourist industry has escalated just in the past 20 years. Restaurants, hotels, attractions, ski resorts, and other visitor amenities have been installed. The future task of Boone is to allow and regulate development in such a way that the scenery and mountains are not adversely affected by tourism. Folks here claim not to want to become another Gatlinburg—they'd rather visit there and come home to relatively low-density development and open spaces here. It remains to be seen if this delicate balance can be achieved by community leaders and politicians.

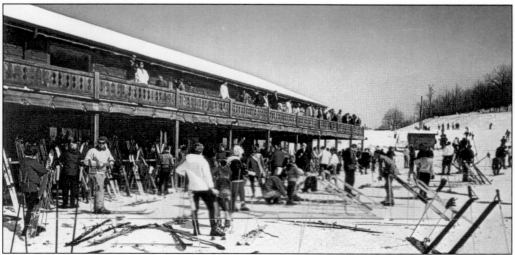

BLOWING ROCK SKI LODGE. This 1957 photograph taken by Hugh Morton, owner of Grandfather Mountain, shows the beginnings of the ski industry in the mountains. Blowing Rock Ski Lodge was one of the first ski resorts here and is now Appalachian Ski Mountain. After snow-making technology arrived, numerous ski resorts have been developed near Banner Elk, Beech Mountain, and Avery County. The resorts are the only draw up here for tourists in the winter, and they contribute substantially to the economy. (Courtesy Brian Lambeth.)

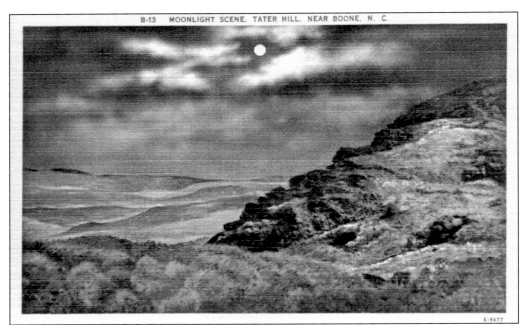

TATER HILL MOONLIGHT SCENE NEAR BOONE. This *c.* 1940 postcard shows the beautiful landscape surrounding the area. This area is located near the Blue Ridge Parkway, which passes by nearby Blowing Rock. (Courtesy Appalachian Cultural Museum.)

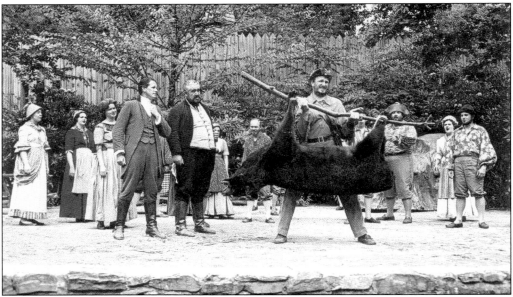

DANIEL BOONE IN THE *HORN IN THE WEST* OUTDOOR DRAMA. This 1957 photograph by Hugh Morton shows a popular summer event in Boone. Pictured from left to right, in the front row, are Bill Ross, Charlie Elledge, and Glenn Causey. The drama has been staged since 1952 at the Hickory Ridge Homestead. Hickory Ridge includes restored log cabins and portrays frontier life in the mountains. The drama and the homestead rely on mostly volunteer assistance and hope to continue into the future. (Courtesy Brian Lambeth.)

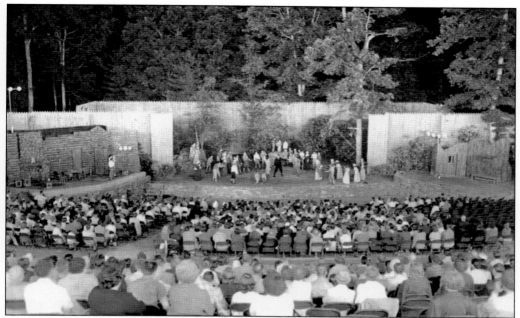

DANIEL BOONE THEATRE. This 1972 postcard reads, "The amphitheatre is located in a natural forest setting once dear to the man whose name it bears. Kermit Hunter's *Horn in the West* features Daniel Boone and plays nightly during summer months." The drama is attended by thousands of visitors during the summer. (Courtesy Brian Lambeth.)

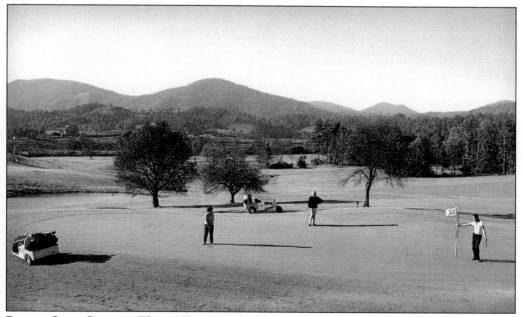

BOONE GOLF COURSE. This 1957 postcard of beautiful Boone Golf Course was produced by Hugh Morton. The view shows the changing fall foliage to advantage. This course is considered to be one of the highest quality public golf courses in the region. It was developed in 1959 by Wade Brown (pictured on page 117). (Courtesy Brian Lambeth.)

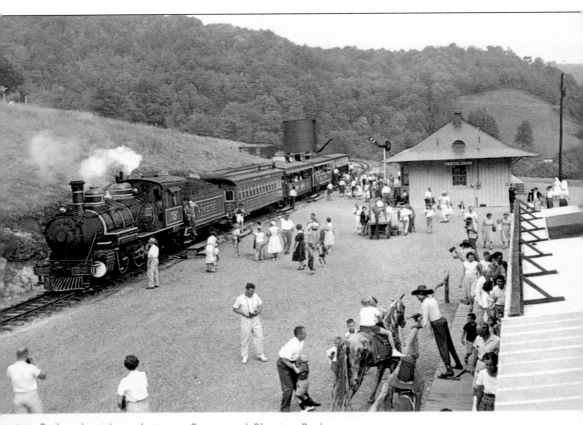

veetsie Railroad, midway between Boone and Blowing Rock

TWEETSIE RAILROAD MIDWAY BETWEEN BOONE AND BLOWING ROCK. Tweetsie Railroad theme park got its start with Grover Robbins. Mr. Robbins bought the old Tweetsie Railroad Locomotive #12 from a tourist park in Harrisonburg, Virginia and brought it home. The park was named Tweetsie after the East Tennessee and Western North Carolina Railroad line, which ran through Boone. The trains along the line were nicknamed Tweetsie because of their piercing, lonesome whistle. After the rail was discontinued, residents said they missed the "tweet" of the train whistle. Tweetsie went on its first run on July 4, 1957. The three-mile track around the park has been reconstructed. Millions of children and adults have experienced this western theme park, including the author as a child. The park is an asset to the area and is still open today. This photograph was taken by Hugh Morton in 1957. (Courtesy Brian Lambeth.)

TWEETSIE RAILROAD. This 1966 postcard shows the train rounding the curve. One can almost the hear the lonesome whistle blow, which is how Tweetsie got its name. Tweetsie Railroad theme park has been open since 1957 and is located between Boone and Blowing Rock on U.S. Highway 321. (Courtesy Appalachian Cultural Museum.)

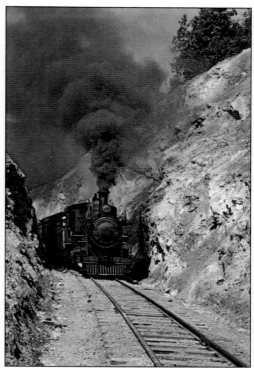

THE BLOWING ROCK. This visible outcrop is the source of the name for the town of Blowing Rock. The rock has been an attraction since the early 1900s. It's said that light objects thrown from the rock will be blown back by the wind from John's River Gorge below. The Rock was included in the 1940s *Ripley's Believe It or Not* column as "The place it snowed upside down." The Blowing Rock is open for visitors. (Courtesy Jerry Burns, with *The Blowing Rocket*.)

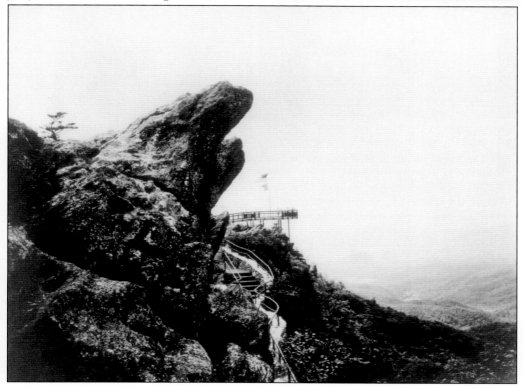

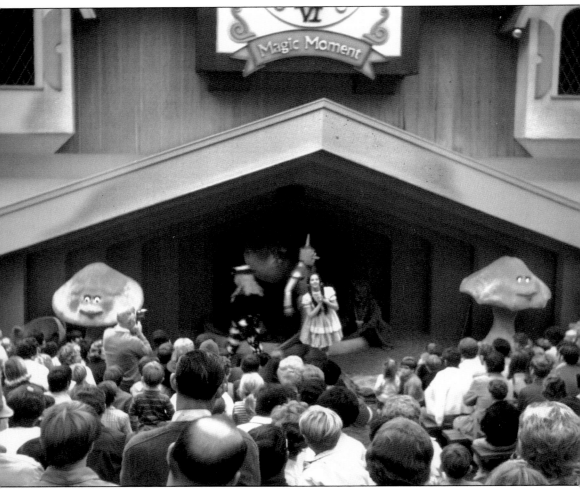

THE LAND OF OZ. The Land of Oz, located on top of Beech Mountain, was developed by Grover and Harry Robbins. The park was a top tourist destination in North Carolina, and in 1970 it received an award as the best new tourist attraction in America. Talking mushrooms, and (of course) Dorothy and her friends provided entertainment for thousands. The park was closed in 1980 and only remnants of the yellow brick road remain above Ski Beech resort. Recently, the Emerald Mountain Development has planned home sites around the park and has restored Dorothy's farm and some of the park elements. (Courtesy *The Blowing Rocket*.)

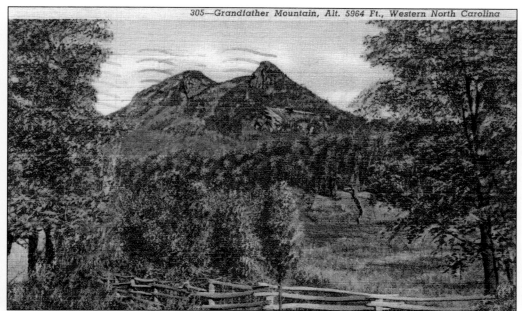

GRANDFATHER MOUNTAIN. This card shows a major attraction in North Carolina since the 1940s, Grandfather Mountain. The mile-high swinging bridge, nature park, and trails are the visitor's reward after driving up the steep access road. Postmarked 1946, this card is addressed to Mr. F.B. Ticknor in Washington, D.C., and reads "Greyhound lv. Wash. 5:00 AM—Richmond change—Winston-Salem change—arrive 8:40 PM. But I am leaving Thurs. Aug. 29. Let me know as soon as possible if you are coming so I can get you a room. You can attend classes, roam hills, interesting town. Glad you are o.k. Love Margaret." (Courtesy Appalachian Cultural Museum.)

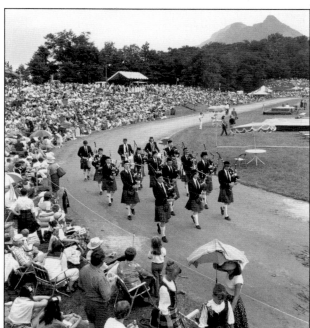

SCOTTISH HIGHLAND GAMES. The Scottish Highland Games have been held at MacRae Meadows on the grounds of Grandfather Mountain since 1956. Hugh MacRae, with the Linville Improvement Company, built a cabin and tower on the mountain in 1936. Held the second weekend in July, this event is the largest Scottish clan gathering in the world. Thousands of visitors now attend to watch dance contests, games, and research their clan history. (Courtesy Jerry Burns with *The Blowing Rocket*.)

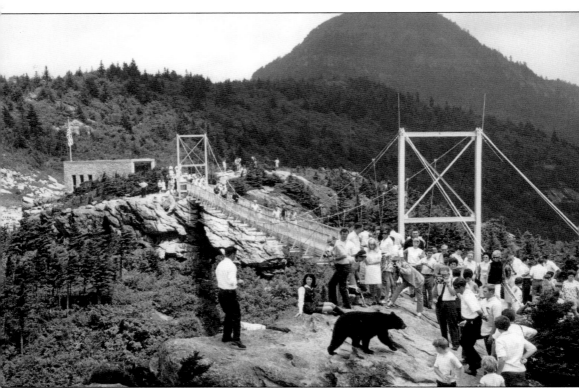

MILE HIGH SWINGING BRIDGE. The Mile High Swinging Bridge has long been a landmark on the top of Grandfather Mountain in nearby Linville. The mountain preserve is owned by Hugh Morton. A road from the 1890s was extended to the mountain in 1935, and the famous bridge opened in 1952. Numerous hiking trails and picnic areas surround the nature preserve. A zoo and museum also draw visitors from all over the country. The Mile High Swinging Bridge requires caution but the view makes it worth braving. The photograph was taken by Hugh Morton. (Courtesy Jerry Burns with *The Blowing Rocket*.)